# GA DOCUMENT EXTRA

We are proud to announce the new series
写真，図面，インタヴューでつづる新発想の建築書

Edited and Photographed by Yukio Futagawa     Interview by Yoshio Futagawa
企画・編集・撮影：二川幸夫     インタヴュー：二川由夫

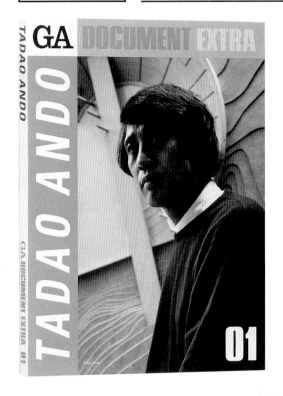

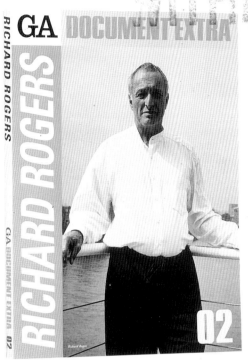

## 01
### TADAO ANDO
### 安藤忠雄

Size: 300 × 228mm／176 total pages, 56 in color
定価2,990円（本体価格2,903円）

## 02
### RICHARD ROGERS
### リチャード・ロジャース

Size: 300 × 228mm／168 total pages, 64 in color
定価2,990円（本体価格2,903円）

## 03
### ZAHA M. HADID
### ザハ・ハディド

Size: 300 × 228mm／160 total pages, 64 in color
定価2,990円（本体価格2,903円）

## 04
### CHRISTIAN DE PORTZAMPARC
### クリスチャン・ド・ポルザンパルク

Size: 300 × 228mm／168 total pages, 64 in color
定価2,990円（本体価格2,903円）

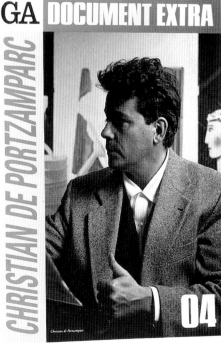

GA DOCUMENT EXTRA is a new series of publications. Each issue is dedicated to an architect and documents the latest works through photographs, drawings and interviews.
Each issue contains three chapters.
The first chapter illustrates the architect's past, present and future through and in-depth interview at his/ her atelier.
The second chapter focuses on recently built projects illustrated with abundant color and black-and-white photographs and interviews.
The third chapter introduces projects currently in progress in order to examine the architect's philosophy for the future.

いま，世界の第一線で活躍する建築家群像に，写真，図面，インタヴューで迫り，その過去・現在・未来を3部構成でつづる新しい発想の建築書——GAドキュメント・エクストラ。
第1章では，彼らの創造の場であるアトリエを訪問。設計の現場をくまなくルポルタージュ。建築を志すに至った背景，どのようにして建築を学んできたか，そして今，建築の現在に向けて何を思うかを聞く。
第2章では最近実現した建築作品を紹介。そのデザインの核心を問い，それぞれの作品についてルポルタージュ。
第3章では，現在進行中のプロジェクトを中心に，明日に向けての建築思考をインタヴュー。

*Ecole de danse de l'Opéra de Paris, Nanterre, 19*

WITHDRAWN

*GA DOCUMENT EXTRA 04*

# CHRISTIAN DE PORTZAMPARC

# CHRISTIAN DE

# GA DOCUMENT EXTRA 04

# PORTZAMPARC

*Interview with Christian de Portzamparc, Paris, July 1995*

企画・編集・撮影: 二川幸夫　　インタヴュー: 二川由夫

Edited and Photographed by Yukio Futagawa　　Interview by Yoshio Futagawa (GA)

*A.D.A. EDITA Tokyo*

*Copyright of photographs:*
*© 1995 GA Photographers: Yukio Futagawa and Associated Photographers*
*Copyright of drawings:*
*© 1995 Christian de Portzamparc*
*Copyediting: Yoshio Futagawa, Takashi Yanai*
*Design: Gan Hosoya*

*Printed and bound in Japan*

*ISBN4-87140-224-X C1352*

# CONTENTS
目次

---

## STUDIO

---

## WORKS

---

## PROJECTS

# STUDIO

**GA:** I would like to start with your background, beginning with where you grew up and went to school.

**Portzamparc:** My father was an officer during the war in Tunisia. I was born in Morocco. I stayed only a few months, nine months in fact, but some newspapers have said that Morocco has influenced my work. The first nine months of life are probably important.

My family is from Brittany, and after Morocco I lived there until the age of six. We lived in a house in the country. My first memory of a place was of the Brittany countryside. I discovered Paris when I was six years old, it was a very strong memory because I was seeing a big city for the first time. I only stayed two days but it was very exciting, very magical, what with all the trains and cars, since I was more used to villages. We went to Germany, then from 1955 to 1960 I was in Paris and then once again back to Brittany. When I had finished my secondary schooling, I went to the Beaux-Arts school of architecture in Paris.

**GA:** Why did you choose architecture?

**Portzamparc:** Well, I was already drawing and painting and sculpting. I discovered a book with drawings by Le Corbusier and became interested in the idea of space and scale. I was also interested in the fact that there were different disciplines within architecture, more than in painting. But above all, at first, I was interested in the idea of space. I remember Le Corbusier's "open hand" drawing in the book. It was like a sculpture in which distance was part of the art. The observer is drawn into movement, brought into the painting. Hence, mine was an aesthetic approach at the beginning. I was probably 14 at the time, and I didn't know if I would be a writer or an engineer, but I was interested in architecture and two years later I enrolled at the Beaux-Arts—already a militant follower of Corbusier and convinced that the old school was too academic.

**GA:** Please describe the situation in more detail. For example, how many students there were? How was the school organized? Were you involved with certain instructors or students?

**Portzamparc:** It was an extreme Beaux-Arts curriculum, in which drawing was considered an end in itself. A competition became just a drawing competition with no reference to reality. The programs concerned centers for meditation in the mountains or houses for kings... There was a huge gap between the school and reality. But some aspects of the school were very interesting. One was the vertical organization of the school. There were probably around a thousand students and all the young students were trained by the older ones and worked on the projects of the seniors. It was quite a good artisanal type of initiation. There were ten to twenty different workshops. Some were large and fairly academic, but others were new, and were taught outside the school. I was in the workshop of Georges Beaudouin, the architect of a beautiful school in Suresnes in

*Interior of office: reception* 事務所内部：レセプション

**GA**：子供のころのことから伺いたいのですが，たとえば，生まれた場所や学校のことなど。

**ポルザンパルク**：私の父は戦争中，将校としてチュニジアに駐留しており，私はモロッコで生まれました。数ヶ月，実際には９ヶ月いただけなのですが，いくつかの新聞に，私の建物にはモロッコの影響が窺えると言われたことがあります。これには幾分かの真実が含まれているように思いますね。生まれて最初の９ヶ月というのは，たぶん重要な意味をもっているのではないでしょうか。

モロッコから帰ると，父の生まれ故郷であるブルターニュに６歳までおりました。家は田舎にあり，場所に対する最初の記憶はブルターニュの田園です。６歳のときパリを発見しました。初めて見る大都会でしたから，それはとても鮮やかな記憶です。たった２日間の滞在だったのですが，私は村に親しんでいましたので，列車や車など，興奮に満ち，魔法のようなものに感じられました。それから私たち一家はドイツへ行き，次いで私は1955年から60年までパリにいた後，再びブルターニュに戻りました。高校を卒業するとパリのボザールへ進みました。

**GA**：なぜ建築を選ばれたのですか。

**ポルザンパルク**：そうですね，私はその頃既にドローイングや絵を描いたり，彫刻をつくったりしていたのですが，たまたまル・コルビュジエのドローイングの入った本を見て，その空間とスケールに対する考えに惹かれたのです。建築には，絵画以上に多様な原則があることにも興味をもちました。しかし何よりもまず，空間という考えに面白さを感じたのです。コルビュジエの本のなかにあった「オープン・ハンド」のドローイングを覚えていますが，それは距離というものがその芸術の一部である彫刻のようなもので，見ていると動きのなかへと引き込まれ，その絵のなかへ運び入れられてしまうようなものでした。このため，最初から美的なアプローチをとるようになったのです。たぶん，当時14歳だったと思います。物書きになろうか技術者になろうか迷っていましたが，建築に惹かれ，２年後，ボザールへ進みました——既に闘争的なコルビュジエ信奉者でしたから，旧態依然とした学校はあまりにアカデミックであると確信していました。

**GA**：何人ぐらいの学生がいて，どのような組織をもつ学校だったのですか。そしてまた，特に関わりをもった先生や学生はいましたか。

**ポルザンパルク**：ドローイングがすべてという，極端なボザール式教育法がとられていました。学内コンペは現実と何の関係もない単にドローイングを競うものでしたし，課題はいつも，山のなかの瞑想センターとか，王様の家とかいった類のもので，学校と現実の間には大きなギャップがありましたね。しかし，非常に面白い面もあり，縦割の組織で，たぶん千人ぐらいの学生がいたと思いますが，低学年生は皆上級生の指導を受け，そのプロジェクトを手伝います。なかなか良い職人的伝授法でしたね。10から20の異なったワークショップがあり，いくつかは，非常に大きく，教え方も主にアカデミック，い

the thirties. A group of students asked Georges Candilis to create a new studio. As you know, Candilis had worked with Corbusier and was involved with Team Ten. At the time he was very busy, but he agreed to start a workshop. I joined as soon as I could. Each workshop was near a library so we could consult beautiful books, not only classical subjects, but also on modern architects such as Neutra and Lloyd Wright. We had access to history, and slowly I realized the importance of this, even though at first I thought it was too rigid and boring.

We had to do analytical drawings of classical buildings but I was the first to do an analysis of modern buildings—the Maison de Verre by Pierre Chareau and buildings by Le Corbusier. We were proud when such initiatives were rejected, because we were fighting the school and trying to

change things; it was an opportunity to assert what we wanted. I think studying at the Beaux-Arts obliged us as students to look for something different, to fight against tradition. The school was very traditional and anti-theory, whereas we read and followed the structuralists. We asked for new panelists, and pushed for the creation of a program of collective housing—things like that. We were beginning to discover ourselves.

**GA:** How long were you at the Beaux-Arts? How did this reaction against the school influence your work or your thinking concerning architecture in general?

**Portzamparc:** I was a student from 1962 to 1968. At the time studies took about ten years. The pupils worked very slowly and we were allowed to work in offices or take time off to travel and chose when to present our projects. Architecture studios

were considered places to have a good time. All the senior faculty would say to us "Enjoy yourselves, make fun projects, your work later will be boring, your professional projects will be boring." We were shocked by this. Sure, we wanted to enjoy life but we thought that the future should be varied and creative. You have to remember that in the sixties architectural work in France was all about the improvement of the cities and the building of the postwar urban fabric. At the beginning of the sixties I believed strongly in the new urbanism. We were convinced that 70% of Paris would be completely rebuilt, creating a completely modern city—at least that was the official plan. Around 1966 I began to do exercises on this idea of inventing new neighborhoods and the idea of sequences which I depicted in drawings and photographs. I was also interested in the relationships between the city and the movies—the city as "scenario." In our architectural vision, the new modern city was pure, clean, entirely of our time, cleansed of the traditional fabric of the city which the modernists had rejected. Le Corbusier for instance saw the old city as a hotbed of dirt and disease, and Baudelaire before him had thought it seductive but also evil. This evil city was to be purified in the spirit of modernism. But I soon realized

*Interior of office: second floor*　事務所内部：2階

くつかは，歴史が浅く，学外にスタジオをもって教えていました。私は30年代にスュルネの美しい学校を設計したジョルジュ・ボードワンのワークショップにいました。ある学生グループがジョルジュ・キャンディリスに新しいスタジオをつくってほしいと頼んだのです。キャンディリスはご存知のようにコルビュジエと仕事をしていたことがありますし，チーム・テンにも関わっていました。当時彼は仕事をたくさんしていたのですが，ワークショップを始めることを引き受けてくれ，私はすぐにこのワークショップに入りました。それぞれのワークショップは図書館の近くにあって，古典だけでなく，ノイトラやライトなどの近代建築を紹介した美しい本を見ることができました。歴史へ近づける道筋が手近にあったわけで，最初は，あまりに堅く退屈なものに思えた古典の重要性にゆっく

りと気づき始めたのです。

　私たちは古典建築の分析的ドローイングをするように言われたのですが，私はまず近代建築を採り上げることにしました——ピエール・シャローのガラスの家やル・コルビュジエの建物などです。私たちは不合格になることをむしろ誇りにしていたのです。機構を変革しようと学校と闘っていましたから，何がしたいのかを主張する好機と考えていたわけです。ボザールで学ぶということは，教えられたこととは違ったことを探すこと，伝統と闘う気持ちに駆り立てられることでした。学校は非常に伝統的で，反論理的なものでしたから，私たちは反対に，本に読みふけり，構造主義者を賛美し，新しいパネリストを依頼して共同集合住宅などの教科課程の新設を押し進めたりしていました。私たちは自分自身を発見し始めていたのです。

**ポルザンパルク**：1962年から68年まで学校にいました。当時，学生は建築の勉強に10年ぐらいかけていましたね。学生たちは先に進むことを急がず，オフィスで働くことも，旅に出て休むことも認められていましたし，課題を提出する時期も選ぶことができました。建築のスタジオは10から15年に亘る楽しい時間を過ごす場所と見なされていました。上級生は私たちに言ったものです。「楽しめ，人生を楽しめ。愉快なプロジェクトをやるべし。君の作品はいずれとても退屈なものとなる。君の仕事もしかり。だから，今，人生を楽しめ」とね。これはショックでした。確かに，私たちは人生を楽しみたいけれど，未来は創造性と変革に満ちているべきだと考えていましたから。

　フランスにおける60年代の建築作品はすべて，戦後の都市ファブリックに対する都市と建築の改善であったことを思い出す必要があります。60年代初め，私は新しいアーバニズムを堅く信じ，熱意を抱いていました。パリの70%は新しく再建され，完全に近代的な都市になるだろうと確信していました——これは少なくとも公式の計画でした。1966年ごろ，新しい住区の

that the modernists didn't really take into account the variety and richness of the city, and recognized the possibility of a modernity would embrace the past as well as the new in modern situations. I began to feel that the modern architect was a bit too obsessive and reductive, rejecting out of hand what is alive and creative—the extraordinary reality of the city, a gathering of different epochs, concentrated and constantly changing. I began to find the efforts of the Modern movement rather decorative, in that they hadn't really understood the real meaning of life in the city. In the films of Godard or Antonioni, on the other hand, people were portrayed in modern situations but in the context of traditional cities such as Paris or Milan. They captured this new situation—the city of several superimpose eras. Godard shows new housing and Haussmann. In Antonioni you have new neighborhoods and also classical Milan. I'm not sure whether this is what caused me to change my mind, but I distinctly remember the impact these images had on me. From around 1966 on, literature, critical theory and movies became more important to me, shaping my understanding of the world and architecture. I began to feel that architecture alone was dry and unrelated to real life in the city. At this time we became more and more politically involved in contesting the old methods of teaching. In 1967 I rejected the idea of becoming an architect altogether. Symbolically, I gave away all my paintings and drawings to my sister.

**GA:** Was there anything particular that triggered this reaction?

**Portzamparc:** I think it had partly to do with the seven months I spent in New York in 1966. I went there thinking I would be working or looking at architecture, but I ended up hanging around writers, poets, and musicians, reading, going to exhibitions. I stopped drawing because I thought pictorial architecture was too reductive. I started writing. By the end of my stay my interests had changed to a mix of literature, poetry and cinema. I now considered architects as technocrats. The city and architecture were industrialized, but the logic of industry was incapable of changing the world. My friends and I were also beginning to realize that the "new" vision of the city was not that wonderful, that destroying 65% of Paris was a silly idea. We were looking for a more conceptual modernity, although we had no idea what this might be.

In 1967 and 1968 I was deeply involved in theory and politics. I went back to school and received my diploma in 1968. Then I quit architecture for about three years, until 1971.

**GA:** What did you do during those years?

**Portzamparc:** I traveled, listened to music, wrote, discussed politics, read, attended lectures and did theoretical work. I didn't have a clear idea of what I would become, but then again, it was an epoch in which it was very chic not to have any particular goals. There was a lot of money in France at the time so this was not a problem. I was working with a group of philosophers, theologians, epistemologists and semiologists organized by Jacqueline Palmade. They invited me to join the team after an interview on the subject of new urbanization and how people related to it— an idea they called "inhabited space." I also worked in design offices, but this was just for money.

I read a lot on subjects, some of them related to architecture, but not with the intention of practicing. I felt that something wasn't right in Modernist theory and I was looking for an alternative. I felt that the architectural avant-garde was behind that of other arts and theory. Ideas in architecture were far too reductive and heavy-handed. During my interview with the research team, the others talked about the house and the neighborhood. The semiologists and psychologists were interested in space, form and distance but they were always

発見やシークエンスという考えについてドローイングや写真で表現する演習を始めていました。都市と映画との関係，つまり，「シナリオ」としての都市にも関心があったのです。われわれの建築的ヴィジョンのなかでは，新しい近代都市は純粋で，清潔で，完全にわれわれの時代のものであり，モダニストが拒絶した伝統的な都市ファブリックは一掃されていました。たとえばル・コルビュジエは，古い都市は堕落と病弊の温床であるとみていましたし，その前にはボードレールが，魅惑的ではあるけれど悪魔的でもあると謳っています。この悪の都市はモダニズムの精神によって純化されるべきでした。けれどまもなく，都市に対するこのモダニストのコンセプトは，現実の都市の多様性と豊かさを全く計算に入れていないことに気づき，そして近代的状況のなかに，新しいもの同様に過去を抱えこんだモダニティの可能性を認めるようになりました。モダニズムの建築家は，いささか過激に過ぎ，還元的に過ぎ，生き生きとした創造性——都市の思いがけぬ現実，あらゆる人が集い，集中し，常に変化しつづけるといった現実を排除してしまっているのではないかと感じはじめていました。モダン・ムーヴメントの努力はむしろ装飾的であると，つまり都市生活の現実の意味を理解していないことに気づき始めていたわけです。一方，ゴダールやアントニ

オーニの映画のなかでは，人々はモダンな状況のなかで，しかしパリやミラノのコンテクストのなかで描かれていました。映画は，いくつもの時代が積層する都市というこの新しい状況を捉えていました。ゴダールの映画には，新しいハウジングが登場し，オースマンのパリが登場します。アントニオーニの映画では，新興都市と古典的なミラノを見ることになります。これが私の気持を変えた原因なのかどうか分かりませんが，これらのイメージが私に与えたインパクトははっきりと覚えています。1966年以降，文学，セオリー，映画は，私にとって，世界と建築を理解する上で前より重要なものになっていました。建築そのものだけではとても無機的で，現実の都市生活には関わっていないと感じ始めていたのです。当時私たちは旧弊な教育システムとの抗争にますます政治的に巻き込まれていきました。ついに，1967年でしたか，私は建築家になるという考えをすべて放棄し，その象徴的行為として，絵やドローイングを全部，妹にあげてしまいました。

**GA**：そうした行動の引き金になったものは特に何かあったのですか。

**ポルザンパルク**：1966年に，ニューヨークで7ヶ月過ごしたときの経験もひとつのきっかけとなっていたと思います。建築を見たり，事務所で働こうと考えてニューヨークに行ったのです

が，作家や詩人，音楽家のまわりをうろうろして，本を読んだり，展覧会へ行ったりしているうちに終わってしまいました。ドローイングを描くことはやめていました。絵に描いた建築はあまりに他のものに転化してしまっていると思ったからです。私は著作を始めました。滞在期間の終わりには，私の関心は，文学，詩，映画が混ざり合ったものへと変わり，今や建築家はテクノクラートであると見なすようになっていました。都市と建築は工業化されるであろう，工業の論理を用いるであろう，そして工業の論理は世界を変え得ないであろう，と。友人や私は，都市の「新しい」ヴィジョンは素晴らしいものではないと気づき始め，パリの65％を取り壊すというのは馬鹿げたアイディアだという結論にいたりました。もっとコンセプチュアルな近代性を探し始めましたが，それがどんなものであるかは分かりませんでした。

1967年と68年の間，私は理論的な研究と政治に没頭していました。学校に戻り，1968年に学位を受け，それから約3年間，1971年まで，建築とは縁を切っていました。

**GA**：その間は，何をしていたのですか。

**ポルザンパルク**：旅をしたり，音楽を聴いたり，書いたり，政治論議に花を咲かせたり，読書したり，講義に出たり，理論上の仕事をしたりしていました。何になるかという確固とした考え

translating these concepts in terms of their own specific fields and idioms. I felt that space and the perception of space could not be entirely expressed in words. To understand the problem of rebuilding neighborhoods you had to understand that architectural space could not be analyzed through language alone.

I read Panofsky and other art historians because at the time semiology was a dominant discipline, but I was absolutely against this idea. The semiology of architecture, the semiology of towns was very interesting but categorized everything in terms of linguistic concepts and was not able to get at what is specific to space and architecture. Panofsky's *Gothic Architecture and Scholastic Thought* is admittedly a brilliant book, but he translates architec-

ture into language by postulating a relationship between the order of space and the order of discourse, but for me this alone could never explains the power of Gothic. Gothic architecture originated elsewhere—perhaps in the notion of light penetrating buildings from the sky as a manifestation of God, which isn't a question of language. We must be willing to admit that there can exist a mode of thinking outside language. The raison d'être for architecture is not to be found in language. When designing a project I think in terms of space, figure, ditance, shadow and light. As an architect, I work in an area of thought which is not accessible through language. I am thinking directly in terms of forms and figures. Yet such notions had never been addressed in theory.

If architecture is equivalent to language, then Victor Hugo was right when he said in the nineteenth century that architecture would not exist in the future because of Gutenberg's invention of the printing press. According to Hugo, the book was such a magnificent new form of communication that architecture, which was an old alphabet for those deficient in language, would no longer be needed. The book would destroy the building and we would never again have to build objects like the Cathedral of Nôtre-Dame in Paris; we would no longer need this type of communication.

**GA:** So in a sense, it was a discovery on your part of the specificity of architecture. Since then, you have obviously succeeded in designing and building in response to this. How did you return to practice? And what were your first projects like?

**Portzamparc:** Yes, these questionings helped me to realize it was wrong to reject architecture. Half my mind was involved with theory and the other half gradually became concerned with building. At the beginning of the seventies I saw that form, space and the visual had to be related to people's lives. Interviews of inhabitants with the psychoanalytical group revealed the existence of widespread discontent with the existing city. But who would be

*Interior of office: archive*　事務所内部：資料室

はなかったですね。それにしても当時はまた，特定の目標をもたないのが恰好がよいと思われていた時期でもありました。当時フランスは経済的に豊かで，そんなことは問題ではありませんでした。私はジャクリーヌ・パルマドゥが組織した哲学者，神学者，認識論学者，記号論学者たちの研究グループと一緒に仕事をしていました。新しい都市化について，どのように人はそれに関わるのか——それを彼らは住まわれた空間と呼んでいましたが——こうしたテーマについて面接を受けて採用されたのです。デザイン事務所でも働きましたが，これは単にお金のためでした。

さまざまなテーマの本をたくさん読みました。建築に関係する本もありましたが，設計のためではありません。モダニストの理論には何か間違ったところがあると感じていましたの

で，それに代わるものを探していたのです。建築の前衛は，その他の芸術や理論の分野の後陣を拝していると感じていました。建築をめぐる思考はあまりに狭く高圧的でした。研究者の職を得るための面接の間，別の研究者たちは住宅と街区について喋り続けていました。記号論学者と心理学者は空間，形態，距離に興味をもっていましたが，これらの概念を常に彼らの専門領域の言葉と用語に翻訳していました。一方，私は，これらのことは，空間と空間の知覚に関わるもので，それは言葉によっては完全に表現できないものと認識していました。街区の再構築という問題を理解するためには，建築空間は，言語によってのみでは分析し得ないことを理解する必要があります。

私はパノフスキーやその他の美術史家の本をよく読んでいました。当時は記号論が流行して

いましたが，私はこの考え方に全く反対だったからです。建築の記号論，街の記号論は非常に面白いものですが，すべてを言語学的概念によって分類してしまい，空間と建築に特有なものを捕捉することができません。パノフスキーの『ゴシック建築とスコラ派の思考』が優れた著作であることは疑いの余地がありません。しかし，彼は空間の秩序とディスクールの秩序の間の関係を仮定することによって建築を言語へと翻訳しますが，私には，これだけではゴシック建築の力を決して説明できないと思えます。ゴシック建築の源泉は他の何かです——たぶん，神の顕現として空から建物内に差し込む光という観念のなかにあるはずで，これは言語の問題ではないのです。言語の外にも思考媒体が存在し得ることを認めるべきです。建築のレゾン・デートルは言語のなかに見つけられるものではないのです。設計しているとき，私は明らかに，空間，形態，距離，影，光によって考えています。建築家として私は，言葉を通しては近づけない思考領域のなかで仕事をしているのです。具体的な形や抽象形態に特有の言葉で直接，考えているわけです。しかし，これらの概念は，理論では決して表現されてきませんでした。

もし建築が言語と等価であれば，ヴィクトル・ユーゴーが19世紀に，グーテンベルクの印刷機の発明によって建築は未来において存在し

the one to relate the dimensions of one building to the next, and give form to place? It couldn't be the engineer, because this task doesn't entail calculations alone. Technological thinking alone couldn't lead the world, even if it was governing more and more of the world. I felt that architecture could begin to approach technology in another way, to be conscious of it but not submerged by it.

My first project was the Water Tower, or Tower of Babel. I was working with my friend Antoine Grumbach, who came from a similar background, on outside spaces for the new town of Marne-la-Vallée. The brief entailed a large cloverleaf interchange. l transformed it into a circle and kept some of the trees. But l wanted something to go in the middle. A week later I saw that they were planning to insert a water tower for some nearby neighborhood. I asked why the tower couldn't be placed in the center of the circle. I wanted to create a monument in the middle of the circle because I saw a need for a poetic landmark there. They called to say they liked my idea and that perhaps I could design it. So I did a project, but the engineer thought it was crazy and rejected it. I did another and another until I had made ten projects in all.

**GA:** What was the basic concept you had in mind?

**Portzamparc:** It was a tank with a trellis for vegetation. I saw that metal spheres were being used as tanks in the United States and that it was possible to do something similar in Europe. Instead of using height differentials for water pressure you have a motor. We compared the various projects and found that this system was less expensive to build but more expensive to run. I kept on designing, and they kept rejecting my designs. But I managed to never let them reject them completely, and I learned to be more realistic and economical in a short time. For example, the last project but one had a promenade at the top

*Working on project*　プロジェクト進行中

ないだろうと述べたとき，彼は正しかったことになります。ユーゴーによれば，書物ということのように素晴らしい，伝達のための新しい形式によって，言語として不十分な古いアルファベットである建築はもはや不要となるであろう。書物は建築を破壊し，われわれはパリの大聖堂のようなものを再びつくることはなく，このようなかたちのコミュニケーションを必要としないだろう，ということです。

**GA**：では，これはある意味であなたにとっては，建築の固有性の発見であったわけですね。以来，あなたは明らかに，これに対する返答として建物を設計し建てておられます。どのようにして実作に戻り，また最初のプロジェクトはどんなものだったのですか。

**ポルザンパルク**：そうですね，こうした疑問を通して，私は建築を否定することは間違っていることに気づきました。私の心の半分は理論的なものに捉えられ，半分はゆっくりと建物について注意を向けはじめていました。70年代の初めに，形態，空間，視覚的なものは人々の生活に関係づけるべきであると考えていました。精神分析学者グループとの住民に対するインタヴューは，既存都市に対する広範な不満の存在を示していました。しかし，誰が一つの建物のディメンションをその隣の建物と関係づけ，場所に形態を与えるのだろうか。それはエンジニア

ではない。この作業は計算だけを課するものではないのだから。技術的思考だけでは，たとえそれがますます世を席巻しつつあるにしても，世界を導くことはできないのです。建築は，テクノロジーに別の方法で接近することができるのではないか，それに埋没するのではなく，それを意識することによってアプローチできるはずだと感じていました。

最初のプロジェクトは給水塔——バベルの塔です。ニュータウンであるマルヌ・ラ・ヴァレの外にある敷地で，私と同じような背景をもつ友人，アントワーヌ・グランバックと一緒に仕事をしました。設計要綱には，大きなクローバー型のインターチェンジも含まれていました。私はそれを円形に変え，ある程度木立を残したのですが，真ん中に何か欲しいと思いました。1週間後，彼らが，周辺住民のために，給水塔を設置することを計画しているのを知りました。私は，給水塔をあの円形の真ん中に設置することができないだろうかと尋ねました。円の中央にモニュメントをつくりたかったのです。そこには何か詩的なランドマークが必要でした。彼らは私のアイディアが気に入り，たぶん君がデザインできるだろうという電話をくれました。それで，私は給水塔をデザインしたのですが，技術者はそれをクレージーだと考え，拒絶しました。私は別の案，また別の案と，つい

に全部で10を数えるまで絵を描きました。

**GA**：心に抱いていた基本的なコンセプトはどんなものだったのですか。

**ポルザンパルク**：植物が繁茂できる格子のついたタンクです。金属製の球がアメリカではタンクに使われているのを見ていましたので，ヨーロッパでも同じようなことが可能ではないかと思いました。水圧のために高低差を使う代わりにモーターを使います。いろいろなシステムを比較した結果，このシステムは工費は安いけれど，ランニングコストは高いことが分かりました。私はデザインのやり直しを続け，彼らも拒否し続けましたが，決して完全に否定されないように心を配りました。短期間に，より現実的に，経済的に仕事を進める方法を学びました。たとえば，この最後の案には，頂上にプロムナードが付いていたのです。しかし，何かの理由で，消防署にこれは禁じられました。何よりもその内側から自然光が戯れるのを見せたかったので，とても残念でした。失望しましたが，私はこのプロジェクトをやり遂げたかったので，最後に，コンクリートの量も少なく，より経済的なバベルの塔の案にたどり着いたのです。

ある時点で，新聞社がその写真を掲載しましたが，モダニストはすべて，それは全くクレージーだと言ったものです。モニュメントは，まさにモダニストが闘ってきたコンセプトである

of the tower. But for some reason the fire brigade forbid me to build this, which is too bad because above all I wanted to show the play of natural light from the inside. I was disappointed but I wanted to have a project accepted. In the end, I designed the Tower of Babel, which used less concrete and was more economical.

At some point a newspaper published a photo of it and all the modernists said it was completely crazy. The monument was the exact concept which they had been fighting. They rejected the idea of theatricality, of an object as spectacle, insisting instead on functionality and efficiency. I had clearly adopted an idea in which symbolism played an important role. To me, it was an exaggeration to say that everything would be better off modern.

Around the same time I built a small house in Brittany for an uncle of mine. It's a fragmented building with a courtyard and a greenhouse. The houses are sunk in the ground and the windows are at ground level with beautiful flowers all around. Some trees were planted later. It was a family holiday house for a family and I thought that in a holiday house you would want quiet and privacy. I designed certain parts for the children, the kitchen and the living area, and another house for parents or friends with a little courtyard. It was my interpretation of a house and garden that would allow all the family to be together but also have their own private spaces. It was compact but also had several autonomous parts. This was the first raison d'être for fragmentation.

When I was only reading and writing I was unable to think about projects. Now, with these two projects which had not been part of my recent thinking, things quickly became very complicated for me. I was asked to write a magazine text on my water tower and this text was very ambitious because I had spent ten years studying philosophy, literature and so on. The text was too complicated—terrible in fact. I realized my thinking had become unclear because at the time I was more concerned with architecture. I gave up formal research for the time being and went back to designing projects.

**GA:** But your researches must have continued to inform your work.

**Portzamparc:** After the competition for La Roquette, based on the exploitation of a Paris block, I wrote about the theory of voids or spaces between forms, a concept crucial for the traditional city but which the Moderns had rejected. In my text I said that the void—the in-between space—was essential to architecture and town planning approaches, and part of the reason modernist urbanism had failed was because it had failed to understand this. Lao Tsu wrote, "My house is not a roof, is not a wall, is not a ground. It is the void between all these elements because it is in this void that I live." This is exactly how I felt during this project. I thought it was important to reinvent a concept of place which results from its surrounding edge. Then I realized that the landmark and the clearings in the forest at the Water Tower served to establish the feeling of space. You surround the landmark or you are surrounded by the forest. Both projects investigated ways of creating a relationship between architecture and the city; how to think about the city through architecture, not through the schemes of the Modern urbanist but not choosing regressive attitudes either. The late sixties, when man landed on the moon, were a time of discovery. The growth of cities, a phenomenon spanning thousands of years, had again become a problem. It was in urbanism—before literature and art—that the Modernist avantgarde first began to be criticized. But the initial critiques were relatively naïve and backward-looking. I always felt that a new way forward had to be found.

At about the same time, Leon Krier was proposing his own alternative to modernist urbanism, through a reassessment of

わけですから。機能主義と効率の代わりに，劇的であり，スペクタクルなオブジェであることを強調するというアイディアは否定されました。私は象徴主義が重要な役割を演ずるという考えを明快なかたちで添加したのです。私にとっては，モダンから離れる方がすべてはよくなるだろうということの誇張した表現でした。

　同じころ，ブルターニュに，叔父のために小さな住宅を設計しました。中庭と温室がある小さな住宅で，断片的な構成になっています。建物は敷地に掘り沈められていて，窓は地上レヴェルにあり，美しい花で囲まれているのです。のちに幾本かの木が植えられました。一家のヴァケーション・ハウスでしたから，そこには静かさとプライヴァシーが求められるだろうと思いました。子供たちの場所，台所と居間のあるエリア，それに，小さな中庭の付いた，両親や友達のための別の棟をデザインしました。皆が一緒に集え，それでいて個人の場所もある，家と庭という私なりの解釈でした。コンパクトな家ですが，独立している部分もあるのです。これは断片化という方法の，最初のレゾン・デートルでした。

　読書したり，物を書いたりしていただけのときは，設計について考えることはできませんでした。最近の私の考えではないこれらの2つのプロジェクトによって，私には物事があっとい うまに非常に複雑なものになってしまいました。給水塔を回想する文章を雑誌に書くように頼まれたのですが，このテクストはとても野心的なものだったのです。10年間も哲学や文学などを学んできたわけですから。この文章はあまりに複雑なものになってしまい，実際，ひどいものでした。自分の思考が明晰さを失っていることに気づきました。というのは，当時私は，建築をつくることに心が向いていたからです。さしあたり形式的な研究調査はやめて，建築の設計に戻ることにしました。

**GA：**しかし，あなたの作品について語るために，研究は続けられなければならないのではありませんか。

**ポルザンパルク：**パリの街区を有効利用することをテーマとしたラ・ロケットのコンペの後，古い街にとっては非常に重要なコンセプトですが，近代からは否定された，建物の間のヴォイドあるいは空間の論理について文章を書きました。ヴォイド——間の空間——は建築と都市計画の手法にとり本質的なもので，近代的な都市化が失敗した理由の一つは，このことを理解し得なかったことにあるというのがその主旨でした。老子は書いています。「私の家は屋根ではなく，壁ではなく，床でもない。それはこれらの要素の間にある虚の空間なのだ。私が住んでいるのはその虚の空間の中なのだから」これは， このプロジェクトを進めている間，まさに私が感じていたことなのです。周縁部から生まれてくる場所のコンセプトを再構築することが大切だと考えていました。そして，給水塔という，森のなかのランドマークと空き地はこの空間感覚をつくりあげる役割を果たしていることに気づきました。君はランドマークを囲み，また君は森で囲まれるのです。どちらのプロジェクトも，建築と都市の関係をつくる方法を探るものでした。建築を通して都市をどう考えるか，近代の都市計画家のスキームを通してではなく，しかし，逆行的な態度をとることもなくです。60年代末，人間が月へ行った年は，発見の時代でもあったわけですが，数千年にわたる現象である都市の成長は問題化していました。前衛的なモダニストが初めて批判され始めたのは文学や芸術以前にまずアーバニズムにおいてであったのです。しかし初期の批評は比較的ナイーヴで，後ろ向きのものでした。前へ進むための新しい方法を見つけることが必要だといつも感じていました。

　同じころ，レオン・クリエが，モダニストの都市計画の代替案を提示しましたが，それは，中世や19世紀の都市を再検討するというものでした。彼は内側に中庭をもち一団となった建物によって街路をつくることを提案しています。しかし，私は，もはやこのような固定した街区

*Water Tower, Marne-la-Vallée, 1971*

the middle ages and the nineteenth century. He suggested making streets with buildings stuck together with inner courtyards. But, I was sure it was no longer possible to build cities with such static blocks alone. Inside courtyards are marvelous in old neighborhoods but even these, if we made them now, would have to be a little different. Our aesthetic and technical ways of seeing architecture are no longer the same. The facade (or rhetoric of the facade) is not a way contemporary architecture can express itself. We need light and views—close-up and long views at the same time. Mine was a new theory of the block. This is a question of topology, of the relationships between void and objects.

I saw the development of the city as following three phases or ages. Age 1 begins with the Greek city and spans all the way to the Haussmannian city. Age 2 is the age of the antiblock and the rapidly expanding city, based on theories emerging in the 1920s and applied wholesale after the Second World War. My own position stipulates that we will not follow either and that we must consider a new alternative. There is the idea of the edge city, but I think we should be thinking in terms of a new city created within the existing fabric, not a unified city but a city of contradictions—fragments of Age 1 and Age 2 thrown together. I don't believe in the ideal city or an ideal model. l don't believe that the har-

mony of the city will come from homogeneity alone. Both classical and modern cities are about homogeneity. In the classical this exists in imitation, in the strict adherence to established orders. In the modern this is achieved by following a rational model or standard based on technocratic efficiency. Today, we have to realize that the city is not homogeneous. It is the city depicted in the films of Godard and Antonioni, which have at least two faces and sometimes more.

I don't think we can afford the liberal attitude which claims that capitalism alone will ensure the city's future, and which simply can't provide the required intellectual tools for intelligent urban development.

*La rue des Hautes-Formes, Paris, 1979*

*Elderly housing "Rue du Chatean des Rentiers," Paris, 1985*

だけで都市をつくることはできないと確信しています。建物の内側にある中庭は，古い住区のなかでは素晴らしいものですが，こうしたものでさえ，もし今私がつくるとしたら，少し違ったものにしなければならないでしょう。建築に対するわれわれの美意識や技術は，もはや同じではないのです。ファサードやファサードのレトリックは，現代建築を表現する方法ではありません。われわれには光と眺めが必要なのです——近景と遠景の両方が同時に。私のは街区割というものに対する新しい論理でした。ヴォイドと実体の間の関係，つまりトポロジーの問題なのです。私は都市の発展を次の3段階あるいは3つの時代として考えました。第一の時代は，ギリシャの都市の始まりからオースマンの都市に至るまで。第二の時代は，街区割というもの

に異議申し立てした時代で，20年代に生まれた論理に基づき，第二次大戦後に広範に行われた急速な都市の拡張の時代です。私自身の立場は，このどちらにも従わないこと，従って，新たな代替案を考えなければならないというものです。周縁都市という考え方がありますが，私は既存の都市ファブリックのなかにつくられる新しい都市という点から考えるべきであると思います。一体化した都市ではなく，第一時代と第二時代の断片が共に投影され，矛盾を内包した都市ですね。理想都市や理想のモデルといったものは信じていません。同質性のみから都市の調和が生まれるとも信じていません。古典の都市も近代都市も同質性に関わるものでした。古典の都市のなかでは，これは模倣や，既存秩序に対する厳格な固執のかたちで存在しています

し，近代都市においては，合理主義モデルやテクノクラート的な効率に基づいた基準に従うことによってつくりあげられています。今日，われわれは，都市は同質ではないということを認識すべきだろうと思います。ゴダールやアントニオーニの映画に描かれた都市，少なくとも2つの顔をもち，ときにさらに複雑な相貌をもつものが都市であることを。

私はまた，資本主義のみで，都市の未来は保証されるだろうと主張する自由主義的な態度をとることができるとも思いません。それは，聡明な都市開発のために要求される知的な道具を何も提供できないのです。多くの都市は今も成長し，建て替えられています。次の世紀には，まったく巨大な地域を変貌させなければならなくなるでしょう。たとえば，日本の都市を例に

Many cities are still growing and rebuilding. In the next century we will have to transform whole neighborhoods completely. I am very much against this idealization of chaos which takes, say, the cities of Japan as examples. I wouldn't say Japanese cities are chaotic; they are cities with strong contrasts and differences. We have to learn how to use this contrast and diversity to create new coherences, new poetics. Men have always feared the chaotic aspect of their cities. Yet in Rome,

Sixtus V exploited this to invent Baroque urbanism.

My theory calls for a case-by-case approach, in which we react to each specific place and time. We have to relate today's city to that of tomorrow, and not to a city whose raison d'être has changed. The world of the car and the television and the supermarket and the fax has changed a lot of things. We have to balance the old and the new. I had all these ideas but it was very difficult to construct a coherent the-

ory out of them. Instead, I learned from each project and the situations they entailed, balancing abstract thought and real experience, and now I understand the theoretical reasons why I tackled the city block in this way.

**GA:** What about the aesthetic of your architecture? It may not be purely a question of aesthetics, but an approach to spatial effects. To me your work has changed gradually since the seventies. Can you analyze this shift for me? Is it in part a response to

*Ecole de danse de l'Opera de Paris, Nanterre, 1987*

あげて，このカオスを理想化することには反対です。日本の都市はカオスだと私は思っていませんから，この読み方自体が大きな誤りです。日本の都市は強いコントラストと差異をもった都市なのです。この対比性と多様性を新たな調和と詩をつくるためにどう採り入れられるかを学ぶべきなのです。人間は常に都市がカオス化することを恐れてきました。しかし，ローマでは，シクストゥス5世がこれをバロックの都市計画を創造するために利用しています。

私の理論は，本質的に，特定の場所や時間に対応していく，ケース・バイ・ケースの取り組み方を要求します。今日の都市を，その存在理由が変わってしまった都市ではなく，明日の都市へと結びつけなければならないのです。自動車，テレビ，スーパーマーケット，ファックス

の世界は多くのことを変えてしまいました。古いものと新しいものの均衡をとらねばなりません。こうした考えをもっていましたが，それらから一貫した理論を構築することは非常に難しいことでした。その代わりに，それぞれのプロジェクトと，それらが引き起こす状況，抽象的思考と現実の経験とのバランスをとるということから学んできたのです。そして，今，街区について何故自分がこの方法で取り組んだのか，その論理的理由が納得できました。

**GA：**あなたの建築の美学はどういうものなのですか。純粋に美学の問題ではなく，空間的な効果に対する取組み方なのかもしれませんが。私には，あなたの作品が1970年代からゆっくりと変化してきているように思えます。この転換について分析して下さいませんか。それは商業

的要求に対する応答でもあるのでしょうか。

**ポルザンパルク：**形態と美学についての問題は論じるのが難しいですね。論じ合うのを常に避けているという意味ではなく，むしろ逆に，私は仕事のチームとよく話し合いますし，なぜ他ではなくこの方法をとるのかについて説明しようとつとめています。しかし私の作品は，空間というものと，言葉で表現できるものとを明快に区別しようというものなのです。空間の質を表現する必要は理解できますし，明らかに筋の通ったことです。しかし，私は，目に見える純粋な形をとり，客観的に正当化することのできない，作品のこうした局面が消え去らないように注意しています。これはどんな芸術作品にも見つけることのできるものです。ソル・ルウィットのような人は，物が何故ある方法でつくら

commercial demands?

**Portzamparc:** The question of form and aesthetics is difficult to discuss. I don't mean to say that I always avoid discussing it; on the contrary, I speak a lot with my team and try to explain why I approach things in certain ways and not in others. But my work does try to distinguish between what is space and what can be expressed in language. The need to express the quality of a space is understandable and clearly reasonable. But I take care not to eliminate those aspects of a work which take purely the form of the visible, and which can't be justified objectively. This is something you find in any artistic work. Somebody like Sol Lewitt can explain why things were made a certain way, but sometimes he would say these things are better left unexplained. In architecture we are obliged to explain things because the work is so closely linked to society. But, from the beginning I have always felt that space can work without being completely rationalized. A good building contains a lot more than any comment in language, and more than what authors can do or say.

My aesthetic choices, however, never relate to commercial pressures.

**GA:** So you never take the demands of fashion into account in your programs. But architecture moves with the world, the world of commerce—like art or fashion. Do you ever think of it in these terms?

**Portzamparc:** Perhaps, but not consciously.

*"Le Croissant," Marne-la-Vallée, 1985*

れるのか説明することができますが，時には，説明しないでおく方がよいと言うでしょう。建築においては，それが社会と密接に結びついているゆえに，それを説明する義務があります。しかし，最初から私は，空間というものは，完全に合理的であることなしに有効に作用させることができると感じていました。良い建物は，言葉で説明し得る以上の多くのものを内包しているものです。

私の美的選択は商業主義やそういった類のものとは，まったく無関係です。

**GA：**では，ファッションが要求するものをプログラムのなかで考慮されることはないわけですね。しかし，建築は商業的な世界と共に動いています——アートやファッションのように。これについて考えられたことがありますか。

**ポルザンパルク：**たぶん，でも無意識のうちにですね。

**GA：**たぶん，無意識レベルでは，外の世界のもつ好みと繋がっていると思います。

**ポルザンパルク：**もちろんです。私たちはすべてそうです。しかし，私たちはまた個人的な夢とも関わっています。たとえば，私の設計した給水塔は一つの夢から生まれているのです。何年か前，私の作品は皆，社会のテイストよりもむしろ文化的形態的存在としての建築という考えに関わる進展を反映していることに気づきました。空間を決定するものとしての建築という考え方です。私は，他の方法よりむしろ空間との関係のうえでオブジェをデザインすると言っていいでしょう。これらの関係のなかで，私は常に，前述した老子の言葉を心にとどめています。ヨハン・セバスチアン・バッハのような体系の構築者に憧れているのですが，私はそういうタイプではありません。私の作品はむしろ，ピカソ的，あるいはフランク・ロイド・ライト的でさえあります。その時代と時の経過に応じて生涯に亙って成長を続ける人たちに近いのです。世紀末のライトがおり，アールデコのライトがおり，50年代モダニズムのライトがいます。超人的な人物です。彼は常に自分自身でありつづけながら，時代の要請に対応し損ねたことがありません。ピカソもそうですね。体系の構築者に対するに彼らは旅人なのです。私の作品のなかには体系に属する何かがありますが，形態が進んでいく限り，私は常に前進していきたいのです。理想的様式というものを崇めないようにしていますし，難しくはありますが，自分自

**GA:** Perhaps you relate to outside tastes on an unconscious level.

**Portzamparc:** Of course. We all do. But we also relate to personal dreams. The water tower, for example, came to me in a dream. A few years ago I realized all my projects reflect an evolution, related not so much to taste but to the idea of architecture as a cultural and formal presence. An idea of architecture as determining space. I would say I design objects in relation to space rather than the other way around. In these terms, l am always keep in mind the Lao Tsu text I mentioned before. I admire people who were system-builders like Johann Sebastian Bach. But I am not like them. My example would be like Picasso or even Frank Lloyd Wright, people who

evolved throughout their lives, relating to time and its passing. You have the Wright of the turn of the century, and then you have the Wright of art deco and the Wright of fifties' modernism. Extraordinary. He was always himself but he never failed to respond to the problems of his time. The same goes for Picasso. They were travelers as opposed to system-builder. Some things in my work are systematic, but as far as form goes, I like to be constantly evolving. I try to avoid worshipping an ideal style, and am always trying to escape my own mannerisms—which can be difficult.

**GA:** Are you saying that you don't have a particular style?

**Portzamparc:** I don't know exactly what style is for me. I don't have the distance of

a critic. I just try to resolve problems and answer new questions regularly. I know style is related to space and I know it's made up of sculptural elements. But I try to distance myself from this stylistic aspect of working, not only to avoid my own tricks but also because I think its more fun to accept change. Some of my projects from the eighties are more in motion and more colored, and correspond to modulations I found existing in the city. We have very strong orthogonal buildings and some which are made of thousands of little diverse components I wanted to include this in my work and not get stuck in a geometrical type of style. That's what I meant when I mentioned Picasso. Perhaps I can speak about style if you ask me about a specific project, for example the Cité de la Musique. I can explain why I chose certain forms for two or three reasons—acoustics, visual factors, monumentality, external geometry, structure, and so on. It's hard to say what is beautiful and what isn't. Some people have told me that parts of my buildings are beautiful and some not.

**GA:** Totally opposing views, then.

**Portzamparc:** Totally opposing views, yes. Some say that my tower at Lille is the beginning of my real architectural work and some say they love everything except Lille. For me, Lille is clearly a part of my

*Music conservatory and housing, Paris, 1985*

身がマンネリに陥らないように努めています。

**GA**：特定の様式をもたないということですか。

**ポルザンパルク**：私のスタイルが何なのか正確には分かりませんし、批評とも距離を置いていません。問題を解決し、新たな問いにきちんと答えるようにしているだけです。スタイルが空間に関係していることも知っていますし、それが、彫刻的エレメントでつくられていることも知っています。作品のこうした様式的な局面からは距離を置くようにしています。自分の癖を避けるためばかりでなく、変化を受け入れる方が面白いですから。80年代からのプロジェクトのいくつかは、前より動きや色彩が豊かなものになっていますが、これは街で見つけた抑揚ともいうべきものに対応したものです。パリには非常に強い直行性をもつ建物があり、いくつかは幾千もの小さな違った部品でできています。私の建物にこれを採り入れ、幾何学的なスタイ

ルに固まらないようにしたいと思いました。前にピカソについて述べたのはこの意味でなのです。たぶん、音楽都市などの特定のプロジェクトについて尋ねてくれれば、様式について話すことができます。なぜ私が2，3の理由で、つまり音響的な面、視覚的なもの、モニュメンタリティ、外部のジオメトリー、構造などの理由で、ある形態を選んだのか説明できます。何が美しいか、何が美しくないかを言うのは難しいことです。ある人々はこの建物のある部分は美しいし、ある部分は美しくないと私に言っています。

**GA**：正反対の意見ですね。

**ポルザンパルク**：正反対のね。ある人々は、リールのタワーを私にとって真の建築作品の始まりだと言いますし、ある人々はリールを除いて私の作品のすべてが好きだと言います。私にはリールは明らかに私の発展過程の一部ですし、

その形態はもっと彫刻的な性格をもつ小さなプロジェクトの影響を受けていますが、にもかかわらず私のものであることに変りありません。

磯崎新氏はかつて、創造的なもののすべてには隠れた部分があり、この隠れた顔は正確にコントロールすることはできないと言っています。テクノクラートの支配する近代においてこうしたものを都市に導入することは不可能であるゆえに、これは問題であると。これは芸術にエゴの表現であれと望む浪漫主義運動以来の芸術の状況と関わっています。浪漫主義以前、芸術は社会の産み出すもの全体に属していました。建築は都市において、芸術であり技術であるというその位置のなかに、真に居心地のよさを感じたことはありません。生活を向上させるためのテクノロジーに依存する技術者と、神秘を創造する芸術家とに引き裂かれています。私にとって、建築は客観的な責任と、予測できない、特異的で、個人的で、芸術的な熱中で構成されているのです。客観性と主観性の対決です。建築家の仕事のもつ様相は、特定の用途についての論議に身を入れさせることはありませんが、しかしまた、完全に不合理であることはできないのです。

ゲーテは、建築は重力、高貴性、厳密さを育てなければならないが、同意（アグリーメント）は不要であると言っています。同意は劇場の装飾のためのもので

evolution. Its form was influenced by smaller projects of a more sculptural nature but it's mine nonetheless. Arata Isozaki once said everything that is creative has hidden parts and hidden facets that you cannot control exactly. He said this is a problem because the technocratic modern age is unable to apply this idea to the city. It relates to the status of art since the Romantic movement, asking art to be the expression of the ego. Before the romantics, art belonged to society's whole production. Architecture has never really felt comfortable in its status as art and technology in the city. It vacillates between engineering process, relying on technology to improve life, and art which creates the mysterious. For me, architecture comprises objective responsibilities but also an unpredictable, idiosyncratic, personal, artistic application; it's a confrontation between the objective and the subjective. Aspects of the architect's job don't lend themselves to discussion of specific uses but then again it can't be completely irrational.

Goethe said architecture should nurture gravity, nobility and rigidity, but not agreement. Agreement is for theater decoration. Georges Bataille said he hated architecture because it always reflects the logic of authority—that architecture is about power and against life. I feel we are now in the position to reconcile the two. We can represent the order and authority of our civilization, but we also introduce individualistic and even anarchist poetics. I try to avoid Bataille's definition of architecture as the "coat of mathematics," implying that architects force their civilization to have a form and to be rigid. I think now we need to escape this academic definition of architecture and achieve personal expression. The urbanist of the future will have to be a poet and an engineer at the same time. We have to be "true," which is the only way to be personal. We owe society our truth.

Urbanism is not just a question of aesthetics. I always keep in mind that architecture serves a purpose, that it is useful in life. If we want to keep this idea of usefulness not as dry functionality, imagination is crucial. The city is a tool for working and living, but you also experience like a novel—a novel of your own life, or a movie of your own life. This is the work of the architect.

**GA:** Could you comment on the general situation in architecture today?

**Portzamparc:** I am interested in several approaches, several kinds of architecture in conversation with each other. I don't have any ideal model. It's more an attitude. I might be fond of Alvaro Siza, Frank Gehry or Rem Koolhaas. But I am interested in and respect completely different attitudes as well I would have strong differences

*Bourdelle Museum, Paris, 1992*

あると。ジョルジュ・バタイユは，建築を憎んでいる，それは常に権威の論理で満たされている——つまり建築はいつでも権力についてのものであり，生命に対立するから，と言っています。われわれは今，この2つを融和させるところにいるのではないでしょうか。われわれの文明の秩序と権威を表現でき，そしてまた，個人的な，アナーキスト的でさえある詩学をも投入しうるような。建築家は，われわれの文明にある形態を押しつけ，硬直化してしまうことを暗示する，「数学の衣」というバタイユの建築定義を避けるようにしています。今，私たちは，このアカデミックな建築の定義から逃げだし，パーソナルな表現をつくりあげる必要があります。未来の都市計画家は，詩人であり同時に技術者であるべきではないでしょうか。「正直」になるべきであり，これが個人的に成りうる唯一の道です。われわれは社会に対し正直である義務があるのです。

アーバニズムとはただ単に美学の問題ではありません。私はいつも建築は生活に役立つ目的に奉仕するものであることを念頭においています。ドライな機能性ではない有用性という考えを維持したいと思えば，想像力が重要です。都市は仕事と生活の道具であるわけですが，そのなかで，君自身の人生についての一遍の小説，あるいは映画のように都市を経験しもするので

す。これが建築家の仕事なのです。

**GA**：現代の建築状況についてはどのように考えられていますか。

**ポルザンパルク**：互いに会話を交わすような，様々な手法やいろいろなタイプの建築に興味があります。理想のモデルはありません。むしろ一つの態度なのです。アルド・ロッシ，フランク・ゲーリー，あるいはレム・コールハースなどの建物が好みかもしれません。しかし，同様に，彼らとは全く異なるやり方にも関心があり，敬意ももっています。今あげた3人の建築家とさえ，大きく違う面をもっています。シュトゥットガルトで開かれた近代建築展には，グロピウスやル・コルビュジエやその他の近代建築家の住宅が展示されたのですが，印象的だったのは，これらすべてが白い壁に黒いサッシの窓で構成されていたにもかかわらず，同じように見えなかったことです。彼らはお互いをコピーし

ていませんが，そこには適切なエレメントの型に対する共通認識——数年前に終焉をむかえた，様式と言語の共同体があったわけです。今日，同質性は完結してしまっているのです。それぞれの建築家が異なったスタイルをもち，異なった考え方をしているようにみえます。

**GA**：それは問題であると思いますか。

**ポルザンパルク**：ええ，面白い問題です。最近の状況は非常に生き生きとしていて面白く，これは確かに良いことですが，アーバニズムにとっては問題です。統一性をつくることを困難にしますから。古典的な都市においては，建築家は彼の建物が他の建物と礼儀正しく調和するように設計しています。今日では，何人かの建築家が近接して建物を設計すれば，統一性をつくりだすことなど不可能に近いことです。たぶん，後になって，われわれはこれを回顧して，クレージーだったと思うことになるでしょうが，こ

even with these three architects. At the exhibition of Modern architecture in Stuttgart there were houses by Gropius, Le Corbusier and other modern architects, and what was amazing is that they were all white with black windows but didn't look the same. They were not copying each other; but there was a consensus as to the proper types of element—a community of style, a language that lasted several years. Today, we have complete entropy. It seems as if each architect has a different style, a different way of thinking about things.

**GA:** You think this is a problem?

**Portzamparc:** Yes—an interesting problem. The current situation is very lively and interesting and that's certainly a good thing. But it's a problem for urbanism, because it makes coherence more difficult. In the classical city, each architect had his building fit in politely with the others. Today, if you have several architects in proximity it can be close to impossible to create coherence. Later on we may reflect on this and think we were crazy. But this variety marks a moment in the ever-changing history of architecture, and I think it will last.

On the other hand, there is the idea of legitimate forms. It's a bit of a political quarrel to demand legitimacy, you never ask a sculptor about the legitimacy of his forms. Architects are always asked to give explanations because architecture is a social object related to public life. Idiosyncratic architecture poses a problem. You can understand that in France during the 80s, legitimate architectural form meant using simple forms made of metal, steel and glass. This was the official French form. It represented progress and technology—the face that France wanted to show the world. That's why the Cité de la Musique was the absolute bastard of the Grand Projects because the officials didn't think it belonged. After 1988, my project was excluded from the official exhibitions on the Grand Projects, because it did not toe the official line. I'm not against any style, even the glass and steel aesthetic which the officials have taken up. Jean Nouvel's work, for instance, is often exciting and highly individual. But we don't have fight this attempt to impose a given direction. The city is made up of copies of architecture, and not of pure original architecture—which is a good thing. Good buildings have to be the goal.

**GA:** This brings up the fact that nationalism seems to be on the rise in architecture.

**Portzamparc:** Yes, in Berlin for instance, they are promoting a Prussian architecture through the work of people like Kollhoff and Ungers. Architecture has this ability to communicate without language, or better put, architecture can communicate because it goes beyond language. You can understand architecture without verbal explanation, and this is its power. This is one of the reasons monuments were rejected after the Second World War. Our predecessors rejected the use of architecture to express political identity. After the war architecture was supposed to express democracy and progress and the end of totalitarianism. In France, for instance, there were few new churches and almost no major state buildings. The only significant production in Paris was the UNESCO building, the seat of an international institution. Nations repressed their own self-representations. When I built the Water Tower the modernists reacted strongly against it because of its symbolism. But since then the Arch at La Défense has shown that the idea of the architectural symbol has returned as a way to express the times and also political identity.

**GA:** Could you expand a little on what you see as the role of symbolism?

**Portzamparc:** It's something I haven't really talked about since the seventies. The word "symbolism" is complex and open to different interpretations. You have the psychoanalytical interpretation of symbolism. The term is used in semiology and

---

の多様さは，おそらく建築の変転しつづける歴史の一瞬であり，それはいずれ終わるだろうと思っています。

また一方で，われわれには，正統の形態という考えがあります。この正統性を求めることは多少政治的な闘争ではあります。彫刻家に正統な形態を求める者はありませんから。建築は公共生活と関わり社会性をもつ実体ですから，建築家は常に説明を求められます。特異な建築は問題を引き起こします。ご存知のように，80年代のフランスでは，正統な建築形態は，メタルとスティールとガラスでできたシンプルな形を使うことでした。これが公式のフランス形式でした。進歩とテクノロジーを表現する——フランスが世界に見せたかった顔でした。この理由で，私の音楽都市はグラン・プロジェのまったくの私生児でした。当局はそれがグラン・プロジェにふさわしいと考えませんでしたから。1988年以降，私のプロジェクトは，グラン・プロジェの公式展示から外されました。当局公認の方向に従っていなかったからです。私は個人的には，どのようなスタイルに対しても反対していません。当局が採用したこのガラスとスティールの美学に対してさえです。たとえば，ジャン・ヌヴェルの作品にはよく，わくわくさせられますし，非常に個性的なものです。しかしわれわれは，この方向を押しつけようという試みと闘うことはしませんでした。都市は建築のコピーで出来上がっており，純粋にオリジナルな建築——つまり良いものでできているわけではないのです。良い建築が目的にならなければならないと思います。

**GA**：これは，ナショナリズムが建築の分野にも起こりつつあることを考えさせますが。

**ポルザンパルク**：その通りです。たとえばベルリンでは，コルホッフやウンガースのような人々によって，プロシャ風建築を促進させています。建築は言葉なしに伝達するというこの能力をもっているわけですが，つまりさらによく言えば，建築は言語を越えるものであるゆえに，コミュニケートできるということです。言葉による説明なしに建築は理解できるのであり，それが建築の強みなのです。戦後，モニュメントが嫌われたのもそれが一つの理由です。われわれの先輩たちは，政治的アイデンティティを表現するために，建築を使うことを拒否しました。戦後の建築はデモクラシーと進歩と全体主義の終焉を表現しようとしたのです。たとえば，フランスでは新しい教会は少ししかありませんし，国家の大規模な建築はほとんどありません。パリに建てられた唯一の建物はユネスコで，これは国際機関です。国家は自らを表現することを抑制していました。私が給水塔を建てたとき，その象徴性のためにモダニストたちは強く反発しました。しかしながら，その後，グラン・プロジェの凱旋門アーチは，時代と，そしてまた政治的アイデンティティを表現するための方法としての建築的象徴性という考え方が復活したことを示しています。

**GA**：シンボリズムの役割をどのように考えられていますか。

**ポルザンパルク**：それは70年代以後，私が本気で語ることのなかったものです。「シンボリズム」という言葉は非常に複雑で，さまざまな解釈ができます。精神分析的解釈があり，シンボルという用語を使う記号論，意味論があります。ヘーゲルはシンボルとは別の価値ではなくそれ自身を表現する一つのサインであると言っています。私はこのそれ自身を表現するサインという考えに興味がありました。給水塔を設計しながら考えはじめていたことがそれです。建築のモニュメンタルな伝統について考えていました。給水塔は何か他のものに捧げられてはいません。それが意味するものはないのであり，自分を表現しているだけです。さらに，機能主義者の伝統においては，建物は一種の道具として考えられていますが，私には，もし建物が美しければ，単なる有用なオブジェ以上のものになることは自明の理なのです。しかも，機能主義は有用性に象徴的な価値を付与しようという試みだったのです。

Paris

semantics. Hegel said symbols were signs that represent themselves and no other value. I was interested in this idea of a sign representing itself. It is something which I began thinking about with the Water Tower. I was thinking of the monumental tradition of architecture. The Water Tower is not a tribute to something else. It has no *signified*; it just represents itself. In the functionalist tradition a building is thought of as a tool; but it was clear to me that if a building is beautiful it is more than just a useful object, and that functionalism was an attempt to confer symbolic value on usefulness.

Clearly, buildings convey information and generate feelings. They instill fear or pride; They attract or repel you. But their meaning is not linguistic meaning. What it is, is the existence of thought outside language. I have no word for this. Symbol is a rather worn term, though it may convey some sense of what I mean.

**GA:** Perhaps one could use a term such as plasticity.

**Portzamparc:** I don't know if it conveys the notion of thought sufficiently strongly. "Perception" for me is clearly something that informs you constantly and helps you think in certain ways. Texts and talking are other kinds of information-process which activate the language centers of your brain,

but we all have these other centers which are visual, spatial, sensorial. This precisely what I was getting at when I talked to you about the futility of pure aesthetics. Perception is a necessary part of thinking and living. There is this whole other field of logos which is sensual and visual. In the 1970s I referred to this as the visual/spatial. I coined this while reflecting on Le Corbusier. I realized that Le Corbusier was completely obsessed by the visual and the spatial. For him, visual and spatial plasticity was the whole world. The workers would be happy if he could build their green factories and the citizens would be happy if he could built their housing units. He thought himself more important than writers, presidents and kings. He felt architecture was the only true form of the avant-garde in the world. This gave him the energy to write as an architect and explains the messianic style of his writing. It also made him very naïve about society, believing that every one would ask him to build and save the world. In a way, his ideological vision was a Marxist one—an ideology of "plasticity" as the alpha and omega of the world. When I understood this aspect of the Corbusian mind, it was clear to me that what was in question was a kind of thinking parallel to language but not reducible by language.

**GA:** It is interesting that he always said that he was more an artist than an architect.

**Portzamparc:** Yes, he knew that the thinking individual within him came from the fact that he was painting or making sculpture every day. His thought originated in these two activities and found expression as a new city, a new landscape, a new planet, and the happiness of the people. His thought was certainly naïve but it was very strong and respectable. Too utopian perhaps, but noble for all that.

---

明らかに，建物は情報を伝え，ある感情を引き起こします。人に畏怖や誇りを教え込み，惹きつけあるいは拒否もします。しかしそれは言語学的な意味ではありません。それが何であるかは，言語の外での思考の存在形式なのです。これに対して私は言葉をもちません。象徴性というのは，私が意味するものの幾分かを伝達してくれるにせよ，かなり使いふるされた用語だと思います。

**GA**：たぶん，可塑性というような言葉をつかえるのではないですか。

**ポルザンパルク**：それが考えることの概念について十分に伝え得るものか私には分かりません。私にとって「知覚作用」は，間断なく情報を与え，ある方法で考えることを助けてくれるものであることは明らかです。テクストや話すことは，頭のなかの言語中枢を活性化させる別な種類の伝達プロセスですが，私たちは皆，視覚的，空間的，感覚的という別の中枢をもっています。純粋に美的なものの無用性について君に話していたとき，まさにこのことを考えていたのです。知覚は，われわれの思考や生活に必要なものです。感覚的で視覚的なロゴスの全分野がそこにあります。1970年代に私はこのことを視覚的／空間的と題して言及したことがありますが，私はこのことをル・コルビュジエに投影させながら考えていました。ル・コルビュジ

エは視覚的なものと空間的なものに完全に取り憑かれていることに気づいたのです。彼にとって視覚と空間の可塑性が全世界でした。労働者は彼が緑にあふれた工場をつくれば幸福であるだろう。市民は彼が集合住宅ユニットをつくれば幸福であろう。彼は自分を，作家や大統領や王様よりも重要だと考えていました。建築は世界でただ一つ正しいアヴァンギャルドの形式であると感じていました。これが彼に建築家として著作を行うエネルギーを与えたのであり，その文章が救世主的相貌を帯びていることを説明しています。それはまた，誰もが彼に建物を建てることを，そして世界を救ってくれることを頼むものと信じるという，社会に対し非常にナイーヴな態度をとらせたのです。ある意味で彼の思想的ヴィジョンはマルクシストのものです——世界のアルファでありオメガとしての「可塑性」というイデオロギー。このコルビュジエ派の心象の局面を理解したとき，私には，これは言語と平行する，しかし言語によって約分することのできない種類の思考であることが明らかとなりました。

**GA**：ル・コルビュジエが，私は建築家である以上に芸術家であるといつも言っていたことは興味深いことですね。

**ポルザンパルク**：そうですね。彼は，自分の考えが，毎日，絵を描いたり彫刻をつくったりし

ている事実のなかから生まれていることを知っていました。彼の思考はこの２つの活動から生まれ，そこから新しい都市，新しいランドスケープ，新しい宇宙，人々の幸福の表現を見いだしていたのです。それはひどくナイーヴな認識ですが，非常に強く，尊敬に値するものです。あまりに空想的だったのかもしれませんが，非常に高貴なことでもありました。

*Cité de la Musique East Part, Paris, 1995*

# WORKS

# Cité de la Musique
音楽都市

Avenue Jean Jaurés, Paris, France

Client: Ministère de la communication represented by EPPV   Program: West Part—Conservatoire National Supérieur de Musique et de Danse de Paris; East Part—concert hall, music museum, amphitheater, information center, offices, café, housing, parking   Design and construction period: competition winning entry. 1984–90 (West), 1984–95 (East)   Structural system: reinforced concrete   Total floor area: 40,000m² each   Engineer: Sodetec   Quantity surveyor: Sogelerg   Acoustic engineers: Commins BBM (West); Commins, ACV, XU Acoustique (East)   Scenographic consultants: Jacques Dubreuil (West); J. Dubreuil, Jacques Lecomte (East)   Lighting consultants: Jean Clerc (West); Gerald Karlikoff (East)   General contractor: SGE TPI (West); Bateg (East)

**GA:** The Cité de la Musique is one of François Mitterrand's Grand Projects. It comprises two distinct briefs. Your design for the first part, the West Wing was completed first, and the East Wing was completed this year. It seems to me that the two wings are very different in character; the spaces seem totally disparate in intention. I was wondering if this was because of the different times at which they were developed. Does the difference reflect a change in your thinking? Or is it deliberate. Please tell me about your concepts here, beginning with the competition phase.

**Portzamparc:** In the competition draft we had to organize the whole Cité de la Musique, including spaces open to the public and spaces devoted to students. We had to organize these on two sites, on either side of the fountain and the square. At the same time they only wanted one entrance. All the other entrants were going crazy with this demand, I just thought that it was a mistake I decided that it would be better to have the school part on one side and the public part on the other side, because it's very difficult to mix the public and the conservatory. So I had two very different types of problem. The conservatory part—the West Wing—had to have one entrance. All the spaces had to be organized into precise relationships—mandatory relationships between the various parts that had to accommodate the various types of musical activity: dance, jazz. classical, electronic, and so on. The program was developed in close collaboration with the teachers and administration. It's a university, with a large number of studios, many types of auditorium and many kinds of music room. The other side, the East Wing, is for different uses, with a concert hall, a museum, the headquarters of an orchestra, some lodgings, a laboratory for music, and an entrance café, which my wife is working on at the moment. The various elements are disconnected and quite independent.

The East Wing is like a cheese with a large number of holes, or possibly a puzzle. But the geometry unifies the pieces of the puzzle. In the West Wing you have also a sort of puzzle, but it's completely organized circulations that cannot be changed. In a way there are distinctive buildings within the building. For example, in one the public has a choice of entrances, and in the other they usually come in through one entrance. But the two wings are never completely separated, nor were they separately designed. They are necessarily related to each other.

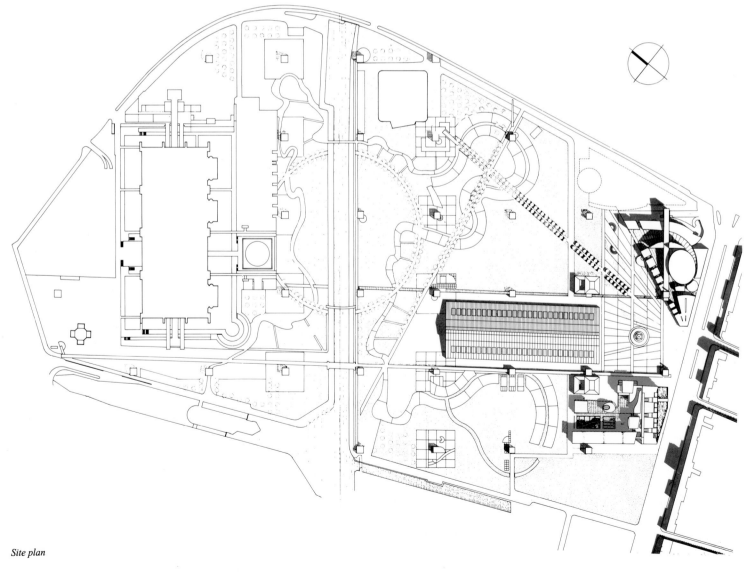

*Site plan*

# West Part

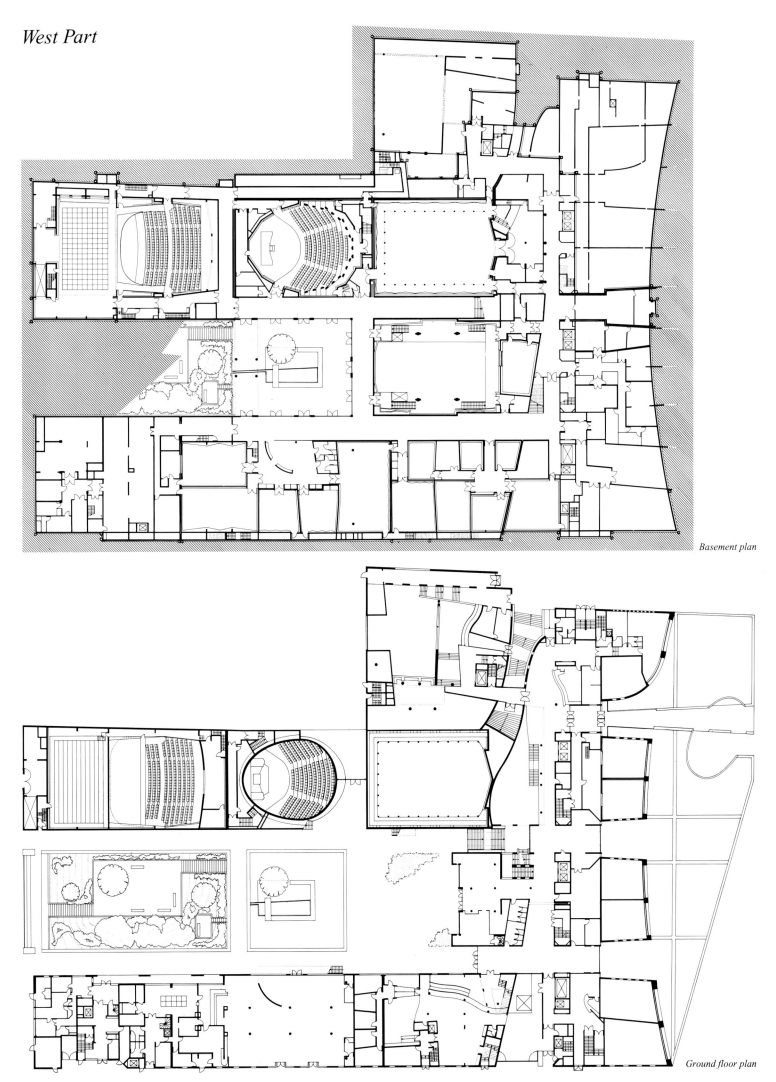

Basement plan

Ground floor plan

*Perspective*

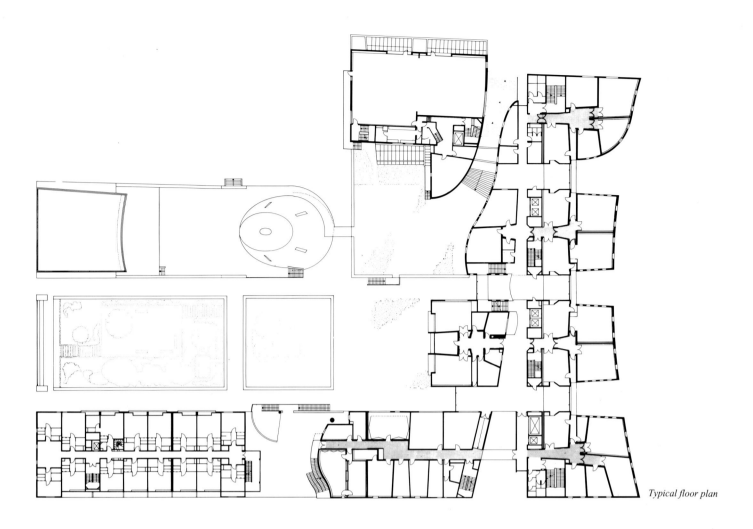

*Typical floor plan*

**GA:** Did this strategy also apply to your treatment of the frontages?

**Portzamparc:** I thought the West Wing was more of an institution and so should be both open to and isolated from the city, with an institutional facade yet ambiguous enough to allow for a sense of surprise. When you enter the building you discover that the institution is not academic at all, but that there's a strong element of plurality. I wanted to play on this contrast between a quiet regular outside and a non-symmetrical, moving experience of discovery on the inside.

You have the same unity of the whole in the East Wing but the West Wing marks the end of the continuity of the Haussmannian city and I used its facade to address this. The East Wing is more like a village between the avenue and the park. Speaking about the East Wing means speaking about the whole context. For example, I had to consider the space of the large courtyard around the existing fountain. At the time there was discussion about whether the front should be symmetrical or not. Only a fortnight before the second phase deadline, in October 1984, we were told that president Mitterrand wanted a symmetrical design, and I thought my proposal would be rejected. I was very worried. All the other second-

phase entries were symmetrical, but I kept my scheme. I felt it important to open the square to the city, and thought a symmetrical organization would be too pompous and castle-like. Nothing in the city or program required this type of organization, which would also have completely blocked visual access to the park. I suggested that the courtyard was no longer an urban square but something forming a continuum between the park and the city. I used the grid of an alley which Tschumi had kept for his park design. So the project combines two axes—one static and symmetrical, and the other dynamic. The scheme was all about interiors and the program, but the problem was also to create an entrance to the park. The explains why the East Wing's entry space is trapezoidal in shape. In the design phase people wondered why it was not symmetrical. But I think this reaction was premature; now it looks quite natural. It creates a condition in which the two different programs are complimentary—the institution terminates the city and the other is revealed in the context of the square and the park.

**GA:** Now that you mention it, the project's open character strikes me as very unusual for a music facility. Concert halls and the like are more often closed, mostly for acoustic reasons.

**Portzamparc:** I treated the problem of acoustic isolation, not in the building as a whole, but envelope by envelope. I believe this is the only case of a conservatory having been designed like that. All the spaces where people walk and meet are completely open, spaces like streets with light and views. When you leave the concentration and silence of a music room you're suddenly struck by sounds coming from far away and you are able to sense the city. Musicians told me soon after the building opened that they enjoy this aspect very much. Most conservatories, especially the big ones, are like bunkers when you walk down a corridor. Generally insulation from outside sounds is treated at the outer perimeter of the building. Everything is dampened by carpet to isolate noise. The dense program, and the fact that the site is very cramped, led me to create what I call a fractal geometry, which means a highly compact building that was open-ended at the same time. The way I handled the envelopes made it possible for light to go deep inside the building. Normally there would have been two slabs with all the rooms organized around one corridor, and the facade would have also been very long.

My problem was economy and acoustics, to use the site so as to bring as much light as possible into the building, to

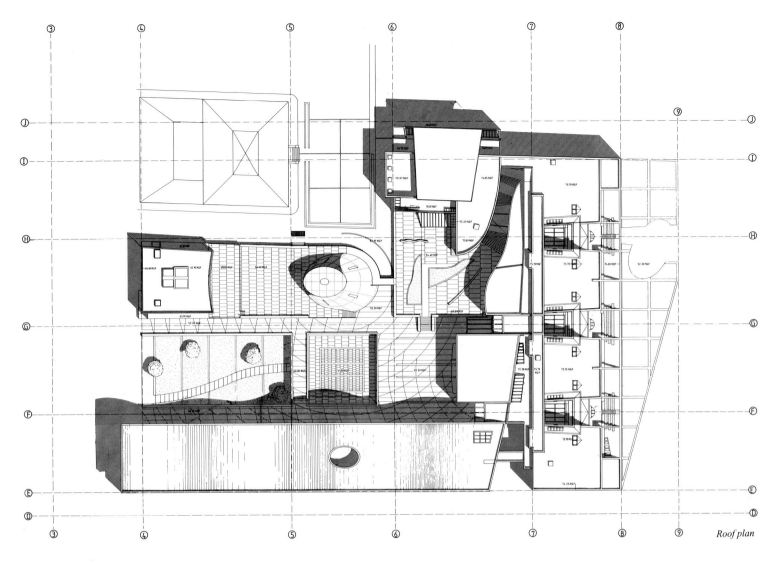

*Roof plan*

**GA**：音楽都市（シテ・ド・ラ・ミュズィク）はミッテラン元大統領が計画したグラン・プロジェの一つですね。2つの明快に分かれたプログラムで構成されています。まずウエスト・ウィングが先に完成し，イースト・ウィングが今年完成されました。2つのウィングは全く異なった性格をもっているように見えます。空間構成の狙いは全面的に異なっているようです。それは，設計の時期が違うゆえなのでしょうか。あなたの考え方が変化したがゆえなのでしょうか。あるいはまた意図的なものだったのでしようか。コンペ段階からの，コンセプトの展開はどのようなものだったのでしょう。

**ポルザンパルク**：コンペの要綱では，公共に開かれたスペース，学生のためのスペースを含め音楽都市全体を構成することになっていました。私たちはこれを，噴水と大きな広場をはさんで両側にある2つの敷地に展開しなければなりませんでした。同時に，エントランスは一つにすることが要望されていました。コンペへの他の参加者は皆この要求に困惑しましたが，私はこれは単なる間違いだと考えました。公共部分と音楽学校を混ぜてしまうのは非常に困難でしたから，一方に学校を，一方に公共部分を配置するのがよいと決心しました。ですから，2つのまったく違うタイプの問題を抱え込まなければならなかったわけです。ウエスト・ウィン

グである音楽学校側にはエントランスが一つ必要で，すべてのスペースは微妙な関係──つまり，ダンス，ジャズ，古典，電子音楽など，音楽に関する広範な分野に対応する各スペース間の選択の余地のない関係に従って構成しなければなりません。これらの構成については先生や事務局と相談しながら進めました。それは，たくさんのスタジオ，たくさんのタイプのホール，たくさんの種類の音楽室から成る大学なのです。もう一つの側，イースト・ウィングは多様な用途で構成されています。コンサート・ホール，ミュージアム，オーケストラの本部，学生用の寄宿舎，音楽ラボ，それに入口にあるカフェなどですね。カフェについては今，妻がインテリアの仕上げをしているところです。それぞれのエレメントは分離し独立しています。

イースト・ウィングはたくさん穴の開いたチーズあるいはパズルのようなものですが，全体のジオメトリーは，そのパズルの断片をとりまとめています。ウエスト・ウィングも一種のパズルではありますが，変えることのできないサーキュレーションが完全に組み立てられています。ある意味でそれは一つの建物のなかにいくつもの個別の建物があるといっていい。たとえば，そのひとつのなかでは，どの入口から入るか選べるし，また別なところでは，主に決まった入口から入ってくることになります。しかし，

2つのウィングが完全に分離することは決して無いし，別なものとして設計されてもいません。お互いに繋がりをもつ必要があるのです。

**GA**：そうしたストラテジーは正面の扱い方にも適用されているのですか。

**ポルザンパルク**：ウエスト・ウィングは単なるインスティテューション以上のものなので，都市に対し開かれると同時に閉ざされ，インスティテューションとしての顔をもっていますが，意外性を与えるような曖昧さも十分に備えています。建物に入ると，このインスティテューションがまったくアカデミックな感じでないこと，そこには多彩な要素が存在することを発見します。静かで規則的な外部と内部で発見する非対称な動きの経験との対比を演出したかったのです。

イースト・ウィングにも全体には同じような統合性がありますが，ウエスト・ウィングはオースマンの都市の連続性の終点であり，このことをそのファサードに表現したかったのです。イースト・ウィングはむしろ，大通りと公園の間に位置する集落といっていいのです。イースト・ウィングについて語ることは全体のコンテクストを語ることを意味します。たとえば，元からある噴水を取り巻く広い中庭空間について配慮する必要がありました。当時，この正面をシンメトリーなものにすべきかどうかで議論が

33

*Section*

avoid a sense of claustrophobia, to avoid long slabs, but also to create common spaces which would very convivial—not too big or open—with ease of access from space to the next. Another aspect was that there were going to be many families of musicians. I used different forms to express these differences in the program.

**GA:** How did you determine the character of each shape?

**Portzamparc:** This characterization doesn't have any literal meaning. This is not how I work. I work on spaces from inside to outside. Parallelepipeds are bad for acoustics, so normally you have to add panels. I wanted to avoid paneling so I designed the rooms with a difference of six or seven degrees relative to the right angle. I either suspended ceilings or shaped them so that there wouldn't be any parallel surfaces. Of course, in addition to the question of acoustics I had to consider problems of natural lighting, sculptural factors,

proportion, relationships between the voids and solids, whilst at the same time bearing in mind that the differences would allow the different groups to have a sense of identity within the spaces.

**GA:** If the spaces are not literal metaphors, then what are they? Do you have an idea of what you consider an appropriate spatial or formal language in general, or are forms always specific to a given project?

**Portzamparc:** Well, in the case of the West Wing I had the idea of positioning four distinct plots within the whole from the very beginning. I realized that the idea of contrasting two distinct aspects or parts came from my earlier work. For my Bastille Opera project, I wanted to juxtapose symmetry with asymmetry. At the École de Danse, I juxtaposed the entry and the dwelling chambers, and was also interested in contrasting lines and curves. It is important not only to consider the specifics of a given situation, but to also

have a clear vision of space in mind. In a sense, this use of axes and counter-axes, lines and curves, was what informed the conservatory designs from the start. The division into four objects reduced what would otherwise have been an excessive scale.

**GA:** My reading was of four regular horizontal volumes with openings and I was thinking that these created another.

**Portzamparc:** I had a horizontal form but it was not so systematic at the beginning. I spoke to Bernard Tschumi about his designs for the park, because he was always modifying his arcade designs. At the time he wanted a simple arcade. In July 1985 he told me he had a sinusoid in his design and I told him I had one in my roof. He came to see my design, and we had a good laugh, but the results were for different reasons. Afterwards, some people said that my design was a polite response to his but it wasn't; it was pure coincidence.

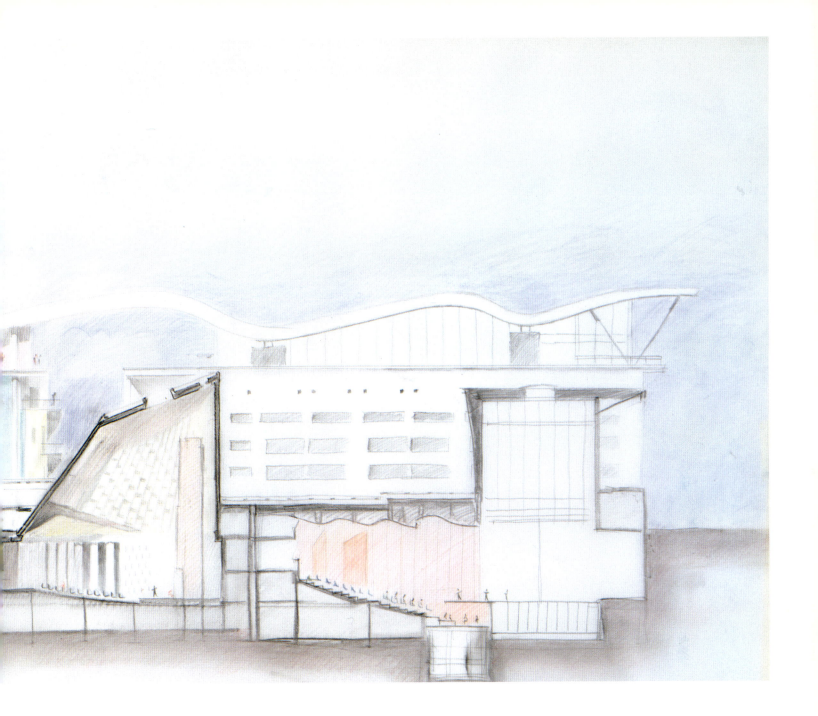

ありました。1984年10月、2期計画締切りの2週間前に、ミッテラン大統領はシンメトリカルなデザインを希望していることを聞かされ、私の案は拒否されるだろうと思いました。とても心配でした。他の第2期案はすべて左右対称性を備えていましたが、自分の計画案は変えませんでした。この広場は都市へ開かれていることが大切で、シンメトリカルな構成は城のようにあまりに仰々しいと感じていましたから。都市もプログラムも、公園の眺めを完全に遮ってしまうこの種の構成を求めてはいませんでした。この中庭はもはや都市広場ではなく、公園と都市の間の連続性をかたちづくるものであることを示唆したかったのです。私はチュミがその公園のデザインに残していた古い小路のグリッドを使いました。それで、このプロジェクトはこの2つの軸線を連結しているのです——一つは静的でシンメトリカル、一つはダイナミックな軸線に。計画案は内部とプログラムに対するも

のですが、公園への入口をどうするかという問題でもありました。それが、入口部分を台形にしたことの説明です。設計段階では多くの人が何故シンメトリカルでないのか疑問をもっていましたが、私はこうした反応は早まっていると思いました。それは今とても自然なものに見えますし、都市の東端に位置するインスティテューションであり、場所と公園に関わるものであるという2つの異なったプログラムを捕捉しています。

**GA:** 今、あなたが説明された開放性は、通常の音楽施設としては非常に珍しいことですね。コンサート・ホールなどの施設は、主に音響上の理由から閉鎖的なのがふつうです。

**ポルザンパルク:** 音響的な隔離という問題を建物全体に行うのではなく、それぞれの被膜のなかごとに行っているのです。このように設計された唯一の音楽学校だと思います。人が歩いたり集まったりする場所はすべて完全に開放的な

ものにしてあります。その方が光や眺めのある街路のようになりますから。音楽室の集中と沈黙のなかから出ると、遠くから伝わってくるざわめきに突然打たれ、都市の存在を感じることができます。建物ができてからすぐ、音楽家たちは私に、それがとても楽しいと言ってくれました。たいていの音楽学校では、大きな学校は特にそうですが、廊下を歩いていると壕のなかにいるような気がします。一般に防音処置は建物の周縁部に行いますから。また防音のためカーペットを敷いているのですべてが湿っぽくなっています。高密度を要しかつ敷地が狭いことは、非常にコンパクトであり同時にオープンエンドである建物、私がフラクタル・ジオメトリーと呼ぶものを案出する結果を導くことになりました。私が被膜を操作した方法だと、自然光を建物の奥深く差し込ませることができます。一本の廊下のまわりにすべての部屋を配置した2つのスラブで構成し、ファサードは非常に長

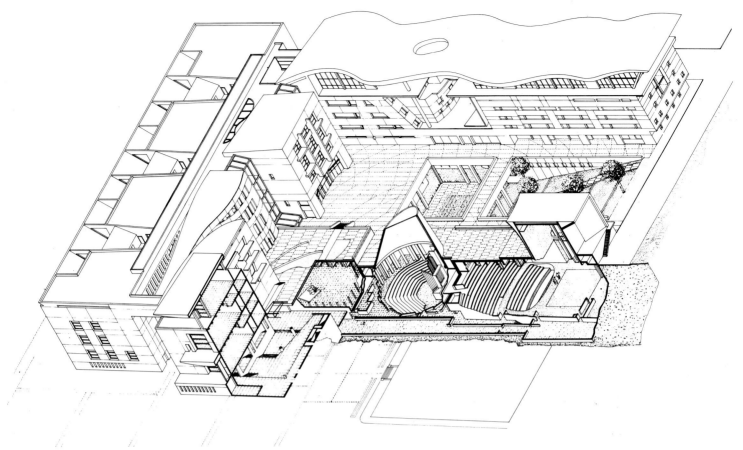

*Axonometric*

いのが通常の方法だったわけです。

できるだけ光が入るようにし，閉鎖恐怖症的な感じを避け，細長いスラブを避け，しかし，とても気持ちがよく，大きすぎず開放的で，お互いにアクセスしやすい共有空間をつくるようにするためには経済性と音響とが問題でした。また，ここにはさまざまなジャンルの音楽家が集まるという面もあります。プログラムのもつこれらの違いを表現するために異なった形態を使うことにしました。

**GA**：それぞれの形態的性格をどのように決めたのですか。

**ポルザンパルク**：この性格の付け方には逐語的な意味はありません。それは私のやり方ではありません。私は内部から外部へと空間をつくっていきます。平行六面体という形態は音響にはよくないので，パネルをある角度に設置する必要があります。パネルを補填することは避けたかったので，各部屋の表面に直角に対し6度から7度の差をつけ，吊り天井や，天井の形を工夫することで平行する面はなくなりました。もちろん，音響の問題に加えて，自然光の問題，彫刻的側面，バランス，ヴォイドとソリッドの関係などにも配慮する必要があり，また同時に，差異というものが，多様なグループに対し，この空間内でのアイデンティティを付与するだろうことを頭に置いていました。

**GA**：これらの空間が逐語的なメタファーでないとしたら，何なのでしょうか。全般に適用される空間的形態的ランゲージがあるのか，あるいは，個々のプロジェクトごとに特定の形態を決めるのですか。

**ポルザンパルク**：ウエスト・ウィングの場合，初めから，全体に対するに4つのプロットというアイディアがありました。2つの明快に異なる局面や部分を対比させるという発想は初期の作品からきていることに気づきました。バスティーユのオペラ座では対称性と非対称性を並置させたいと思いましたし，舞踊学校ではエントリーと寄宿舎を並置させ，また直線と曲線の対比にも関心がありました。特定の状況のもつ固有性について考えるばかりでなく，空間に対する明快なヴィジョンをもつことも大切です。ある意味で，こうした軸線，対抗軸線，直線，曲線の使用は，その始めから音楽学校がどんなものであるかを告知しているのです。4つのオブジェに分割したことにより，さもなくば過剰なものとなったスケールを抑制しています。

**GA**：私の読み方は開口をもつ4つの水平なヴォリュームというもので，これが別なものをつくりだすのかと考えていました。

**ポルザンパルク**：水平な形を考えていましたが，最初はそれほどシステマティックなものではありませんでした。それからベルナール・チ

ュミと彼の公園のデザインについて話したのですが——彼はアーケードのデザインをしょっちゅう修正していましたので——そのときは，彼は単純なアーケードにしたいと考えていました。1985年の7月，彼は私にデザインのなかに一つシヌソイドを使うと言い，僕も一つそれを屋根に使っていると答えました。彼はオフィスに来て私のデザインを見て，二人で気持ち良く笑ってしまいました。しかしこの結果というのはそれぞれ別な理由から生まれたものなのです。後にある人々は，私のデザインはチュミのそれに礼儀正しく応答していると言いましたが，これはまったく偶然の一致だったのです。

それぞれが内部に本拠をもつ，音楽の家族集団というアイディアにとって，スタティックで，対称性をもち，反復するデザインを避けることは重要でしたし，国家的施設という印象を付与したくありませんでした。発見を経験する場所であり，さまざまな音楽のジャンルが内部にそれぞれの場所，つまりこの音楽都市という地形のなかに，徐々に占拠してゆける承認された領土を発見できることが大切でした。この理由で，形態，ヴォリューム，色彩を変えたのであり，それは建物に入ると気づきますが，外からは一体となった施設と見えるのです。内部と外部の経験の間にはコントラストがあるわけです。

また，この建物には合わせて約二千人の人が

The idea of the families of music, with each family having its own home inside, made it important not to design anything too static, symmetrical or repetitive. I didn't want it to be seen as a state institution. I wanted there to be an experience of discovery, and it was important for me that the different families of music find their home inside, their own place, a recognizable territory within a geography, one they could appropriate gradually. For this reason, the shapes, volumes and colors are all different and this is something you realize when you enter, whereas the outside constitutes a unified whole. So you have the contrast between the experiences of inside outside.

Another aspect is that the program is very dense—there are about two thousand people living and working inside. There are more than 150 rooms—some the same, many different. In a way I made these differences more marked than they had to be. The usual approach with a large number of discrete elements would be to use an aesthetics of repetition. I wanted to avoid this idea, and tried to imagine how these elements could work together. I subdivided the spaces so that you would never feel this density of program. Instead you have a sense of intimacy, and the sense that this is a large and great space in which you can

breathe and see things. The ability to determine one's own position, one's own relationship to the whole, the group, represents an important psychological comfort. You can isolate yourself or you can meet people—you can choose. To achieve this, I made the in-between spaces—a spatial network of transparencies, sounds, and light—larger than the program required. I had to convince the clients that it was necessary to make these spaces larger than their function required. In fact, the key criterion for this project was number, or quantity.

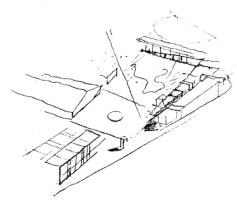

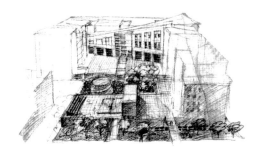

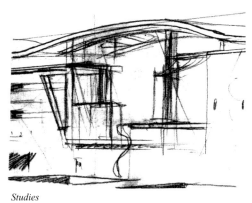

*Studies*

**GA:** I think contemporary institutions, or the way people think of contemporary art institutions, is that they contain less common space than their classical counterparts. Older institutions have more generous common spaces for circulations and lobby areas.

**Portzamparc:** These spaces are becoming smaller for purely economic reasons. We calculate everything very closely and try not to waste too much money.

Large institutions often lose sight of the fact that space can change the way we experience life. Here it's not so much a classical approach involving spatial monumentality that is in play, it is more a question of discovering a network of space through perception in time.

This notion of interior movement is crucial to both sides of Cité de la Musique. My feeling is that they furnish a link between architecture and music. You cannot understand the project at a glance, and in this sense it is absolutely anti-classical. For many people, a good classical building is one in which you can immediately understand the interior organization from the outside. But for me, a good building is one it takes time to discover. It doesn't have to be complicated, but it should comprise a plurality of organizational principles that you gradually discover inside. After the

住み，仕事をするわけですから，非常に過密であるということがあります。150以上の部屋があり，あるものは同じ構成，多くは違っています。ある程度まで，これらの違いを必要以上に際立たせるようにしました。別々に分かれた，たくさんの数のものをつくるとき，最も普通の方法は，反復の美学を使うことです。それは避けて，これらの多様なエレメントがまとまったときにどのように調和し得るかを想像するようにしたのです。プログラムの過密さを決して感じさせないように空間をさらに小分割し，代わりに，インティメートでありながら，一息ついて見回すと広い空間を感じられるようにしました。建物全体に対する自分のいる場所，グループと自分との関係を見定めることができることは重要な心理的安らぎになります。一人でいることも，人に会うこともできます。それを選べるのです。これを実現するために，プログラムが要求する以上に広い，間の空間——透明性，音，光の空間ネットワークをつくりました。機能的側面からの要求以上に広いこうしたスペースをつくることが必要であるとクライアントを説得しました。事実，このプロジェクトの主要な基準は数というより質でした。

**GA**：現代のインスティテューション，あるいは現代の芸術施設に対する人々の考え方では，古典的なそれよりパブリック・スペースが狭く

なっているように思います。昔は，こうした建物ではサーキュレーションやロビーなどの共有空間をもっと広くとっていました。

**ポルザンパルク**：こうしたスペースが狭くなってきているのは単に経済的理由からです。すべてを細かく計算して，お金を掛けすぎないようにしているのです。

大きな施設というものは，空間が生活を体験する方法を変えることができるという事実を見失いがちです。ここでは空間の記念性を演出するといった古典的なアプローチではなく，時間

のなかの知覚を通して，空間のネットワークを発見するというものです。

内部のムーヴメントという概念は，音楽都市を構成する両方の側で重要なものとなっています。これが音楽と建築の間に輪をかけるというのが私の気持ちです。この建物は一目では理解できません。この意味で，それは完全に非古典的です。多くの人にとって，良い古典建築とは，外部から内部の構成がすぐに理解できるものです。一方，私にとっては，発見に時間がかかるものが良い建物なのです。それが複雑である必要はありませんが，内部で発見しなければならない構成原則の複数性を備えているべきです。建物が完成して，生徒や先生は，全体を把握するのは大変だけれど，この建物は大好きだと僕に言ってくれました。毎日発見があり，それが，空間，姿，形，建築の重要性を，自分たちの生活を違ったものにしてくれるものとして理解することを助けてくれると。

ゲーテは建築は凍れる音楽だ，つまり石に変貌した音楽だと言っていますが，この建物はそれにあたりません。私に言わせれば，石に変貌してしまったら，それはもはや音楽ではありません。その関係は，動きや時間の経過のなかでのわれわれの感覚や身体によって建築を知覚するという事実とより関わっているのです。これは建築にも音楽にも共通しています。

*Overall view* 全景

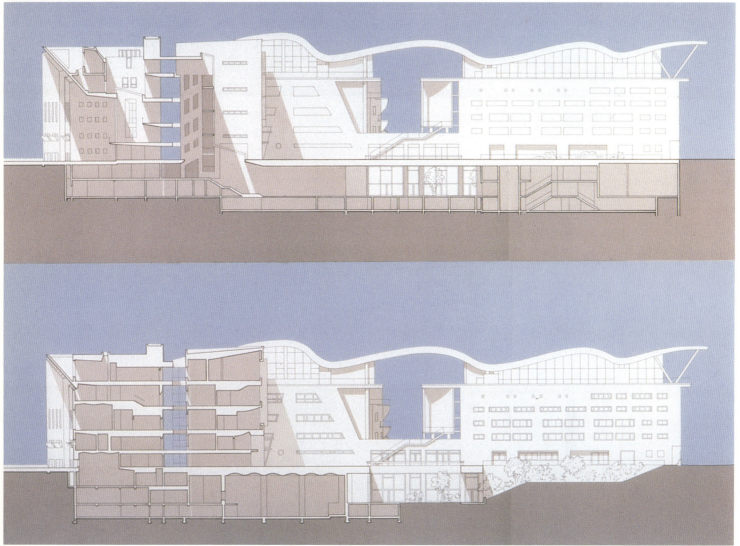

*Sections*

*South facade*・南側ファサード

View from south-east 南東より見る

*View toward student accommodation*　学生寮を見る

*Northeast elevation* 北東側ファサード

building opened, the pupils and teachers have said to me that it was too much for them to understand as a whole, but in fact they like this very much. They say it gives them sense of everyday discovery, that it helps them to understand the importance of space, shape, form and architecture, as something that makes their lives different.

Goethe said architecture was like frozen music, or music turned to stone. But for me, this is not the case. If it were turned to stone it would no longer be music. The relationship has more to do with the fact that we perceive architecture with our senses and our bodies through

motion and the passing of time. This is common to both architeture and music.

**GA:** Some years ago, you mentioned trying to create a musical notation of rhythm.

**Portzamparc:** Yes, in this notion of movement we have to use all the elements to their fullest. I try to exploit numbers in a musical way, with repetition at certain times and change at others. Scale and size, repetition, color, the dynamics of light and shade, and then the larger forms or shapes by themselves are all elements that condition our perception of architecture. I want this perception to be as rich as possible. This in turn raises problems of materiality,

tactility and color. Form is more a question of shaping the void, and this can be related to the musical structures in terms of organization, the passing of time, and even melodic lines. In this sense I've constructed a sort of free movie in space.

Apart from this notion of discovery in space, I also had to constantly responding to precise demands. There is a hybrid of great freedom in the foreground and great specificity in particular places. I took some risks with the circulation system in the East Wing. You see that both sides are organized and based on the relationship between voids and solids, open and closed

GA：何年か前，リズムの記譜法をつくろうとしていると話されていましたね。

ポルザンパルク：ええ，この動きという概念では，すべてのエレメントを十二分に駆使する必要があります。反復したり，変化させたり，音楽的な方法で数を活用しようとしたのです。大きさや広さ，反復，色彩，光や影の動き，そしてそれらがつくりあげる全体の姿，形，これらすべてがわれわれの建築の知覚を規定しているのです。私はこの知覚をできるだけ豊かなものにしたいのです。このことは転じて，物質性，触覚，色彩の問題を発生させます。形態はむしろヴォイドを形づくる問題であり，そしてこれ

は，構成，時間の経過，ときには旋律といった音楽の構造に関係させることができるはずです。この意味で私は，空間のなかに一種のフリー・ムーヴィーをつくったのです。

　この空間のなかの発見という考え方とは別に，細かな要求にも常に対応しなければなりませんでした。最前面にくる大きな自由と特定の場所の大きな固有性の混成なのです。イースト・ウィングのサーキュレーション・システムではある程度の危険を覚悟しました。ご覧のように，両サイドとも，ヴォイドと面，開かれた空間と閉ざされた空間，明るい空間と暗い空間，音に開かれた空間と音から隔離された空間とい

った二者の関係に基づいて構成されています。このプロジェクトを，音の制御を必要とする場としない場とに分けました。公共空間もまたこのプロジェクトの構成に一役かっています。そのヴォイドと平坦な面のネットワークは迷宮的なものです。音楽学校のなかでは，それは直線の連なりのように構成されています。その理由の一つは，音楽学校では，部分とコミュニティ全体の関係が明快でなければならないからです。そこには発見の感覚があったとしても，建物の組立が理解できる必要がありました。それは細長い空間の断片を伴ったグリッドに基づいています。その一つはふさがれ，一つは庭があ

space, light and dark, open to sounds or soundproofed. I divided the project between spaces that required sound control and places that didn't. The public areas also helped to organize the project. Its network of the voids and flat surfaces is labyrinthine. The conservatory is organized into a series of lines. One of the reasons for this is that in the conservatory, the relationships between the parts and the community whole have to be clear. Even if there is a sense of discovery, you have to understand how the building is organized. It's based on the grid principle, with strips. One is filled, one is open with a garden, another contains the different classrooms, and a fourth contains the dance pavilion. These strips can be read on the front. In the East Wing the front is also quite simple: you can understand the plurality of the various pavilions, you can see the various entrances—and then there is the internal organization, which you discover more slowly. I introduced the foyer. This didn't have to be a closed room so I integrated it into the circulation system, the great spiral passage.

**GA:** I read this network of space surrounding the concert hall as an attempt to create an ambiguity between inside and outside. Is it supposed to be like a covered arcade, or galleria?

**Portzamparc:** I was trying to make several buildings in one, in which the sense of inside and outside would be ambiguous—a clear metaphor of the city. But the spiral isn't a literal transposition of the covered street. It's designed to create tension between a dense network of volumes and the public space in between. I wanted the place to be open and alive. The foyers and public spaces of most concert halls are sad and lonely when there is no concert being held. The foyer becomes just an empty room, but there will always be people in mine. There is a bar, computer terminals, comfortable furniture, a record shop, and so on.

The jury probably chose my project because the program was not fixed, and would necessarily change. A typical Modernist response would have been to make a frame or grid to allow for subsequent changes. Here, a grid would not have worked, partly because there are many different users—the building is not unified like the conservatory. The acoustics alone imposed highly specific constraints. So instead I introduced this idea of a sort of puzzle, a topology of planes and voids. During the project we had many discussions with the users and I changed some pavilions without changing others. The open spaces made this possible. It's like

having boats in a harbor. The process of modification continued throughout the project. Shapes changed, and angles changed. This strategy of subdivision became a powerful tool.

**GA:** You mentioned the use of color as another tool in your strategy for enhancing difference. Sometimes your colors remind me of the architecture, let's say, of Morocco, even though you are not Moroccan. In any case, it doesn't seem particularly French. I also wonder whether this was influenced by Corbusian polychromy.

**Portzamparc:** My use of color comes from my painting—something I've been doing since the early sixties. Gradually, this use of colors and sense of materials brushed off on my architectural work. While I worked on the Cité de la Musique, I was also building the Café Beaubourg and École de Danse, which were more homogeneous, more pristine. I may have been influenced by Le Corbusier, though I think his colors are very different. But in fact the experience of space, form and color in sculpture, painting, architecture and the city are all linked. You can have similar reactions to a painting and a building.

**GA:** I would like to ask you about your treatment of specific spaces. You mentioned that acoustic considerations were

って開かれ，別の一つはそれぞれに異なる教室があり，4つめにはダンス・パヴィリオンが入っています。これらのグリッドを正面ファサードからも読むことができます。イースト・ウィングも正面はとてもシンプルです。さまざまなパヴィリオンの複数性を理解することができ，いくつもの入口が見え，そして，ゆっくりと発見していくことになる内部構成があります。私はホワイエを導入したのですが，これは閉ざされた部屋にすべきではないので，サーキュレーション・システムに組み入れ，広い螺旋形の動線通路となりました。

**GA**：私はこのコンサートホールを囲む空間のネットワークを内部と外部の曖昧性をつくりだす試みであると読んだのですが，それは屋根付きのアーケードあるいはガレリアと考えてよいのでしょうか。

**ポルザンパルク**：そのなかでは内部と外部が曖昧に感じられる，一つになったいくつもの建物をつくろうとしたのです。つまり都市の明快なメタファーなのです。しかし，螺旋は屋根付きの街路の文字通りの置き換えではなく，ヴォリュームの緊密なネットワークとその間の公共空間の間に緊張をつくりだすためにデザインしたのです。そこを開放的で生き生きした場所にしたかったのです。ほとんどのコンサートホールのホワイエや公共空間は，そこで音楽会が開か

れていないときは，とても寂しく人気のない場所になっています。ホワイエはただの空っぽの空間になってしまいますが，私の建物では常に人がいる場所になるでしょう。バーがあり，コンピュータの端末があり，心地よい家具があり，レコードショップなどがあります。

審査員はたぶん，プログラムが固定されていず，必要があれば変更できると考えて，私の案を選んだのでしょう。近代建築の，典型的な解答は，後で変更可能なフレームやグリッドをつくることでした。ここでは，グリッドは機能しません。一つには多くの異なった使い手がいるからで，それは音楽学校のように一体化し得ないのです。音響一つだけでもかなりの固有性が必要なのです。そこで，その代わりに，一種のパズル，面とヴォイドによるトポロジーというアイディアを導入しました。設計の間，われわれは使い手の側と何度も話し合いを行い，私は他を変えずにいくつかのパヴィリオンを変更したのですが，オープン・スペースがこれを可能にしてくれました。港にボートをつなぐのに似ています。この修正プロセスはプロジェクトを進める間ずっと続き，形が変わり，角度が変わりました。この再分割というストラテジーは有力な道具になりました。

**GA**：色彩の使い方は，差異を強調するストラテジーのなかのもう一つの道具であるとおっし

ゃいました。ときどき，あなたの色彩からモロッコの建築を連想させられます。モロッコの方ではないわけですが。いずれにしろ，特にフランス的なものには見えません。また，これはコルビュジエ風の多色画法なのだろうかとも思うのですが。

**ポルザンパルク**：私の色彩の使い方は，60年代の初めから描いていた絵からきているのです。この色彩や材料に対する感覚は徐々に私の建築作品から追い払われてきています。音楽都市を進めていたとき，同時に，それより均質的で純粋な，カフェ・ボーブールと舞踊学校の仕事もしていました。色の性格はまったく違っていると思いますが，コルビュジエの影響があるかもしれません。しかし事実，彫刻，絵画，建築，都市での空間，形，色彩の経験は皆一つに繋がっているのです。絵の前と建物の前では同じような反応を抱くことができるわけですから。

**GA**：特定の空間の扱いについておたずねしたいのですが。各部屋のトポロジーを決めるにあたって，音響に対する配慮が重要であったとおっしゃいました。特定の部屋を公共領域から切り離すなどですね。音響上の問題が形態を決めるのに大きく作用していることは確かですが，同時に建築的なヴィジョンももたれていたに違いありません。たとえばコンサートホールについてはいかがでしょうか。

*Drawing: void space*

important in your treatment of the topology of rooms—isolating particular rooms from the public areas. I'm sure acoustic problems had a lot to do with your formal solutions, but at the same time you must have had an architectural vision. Could you address this question with specific reference to the concert hall?

**Portzamparc:** In general, acousticians ask architects to adapt their designs to the shoebox type of concert hall. Shoeboxes are easier to dimension and avoid poor acoustics, though they may not be able to achieve great acoustics.

I knew that a very large volume was riskier than relying on the shoebox, but I thought there was potential for better sound. When you have a large number of musicians, you need a large hall. I had discussions with Pierre Boulez, one of the future users of the facility, and he said he was also suspicious of the shoebox. I decided this was not the way to go. But when I proposed an ellipse he asked me to revert to the rectangle.

In the second phase we were asked to design a classical symphony hall, and I followed the suggestions of the acousticians. But I didn't like it at all. It was a flat hall with a low ceiling for shorter sound reflection, but I didn't like it as space. I decided to change acousticians. There

were three things I wanted to do: I wanted a ceiling fifteen meters high, to have some of the audience seated in galleries, and to use a conic form for the spatial composition. To avoid long sound reflection I reverted to my first intuition, a square and a cone. This developed into a rectangle and an ellipse. I used the rectangle—the lower part of the hall—to manipulate lateral sound reflections. A series of specially dimensioned panels were designed for this, and they work very well.

Boulez then asked for a flat ground and

said he was not against the idea of gallery seating. The balconies contain fixed seats, whereas the ground seats are easily moveable. For me the richness of the ellipse consists in the fact that you can use the long axis and the short axis to create different geometries and different possible configurations. Since the opening in January they have altered seating and stage configurations every week.

**GA:** You told me that initially you had an inverse-shaped hall. Did you keep this idea for the exterior?

*View from west: gymnasium on top*　西より見る：最上階は体育館

ポルザンパルク：一般に音響技術者は，建築家に靴箱型のコンサートホールを設計するように望みます。靴箱型ですとディメンションを決めるのも簡単ですし，悪い音響になることを避けられますが，素晴らしい音響を生むことはできないかもしれません。

大空間をつくることは，靴箱型に頼るより危険であることを承知していましたが，より素晴らしい音を得られる可能性もあります。大勢の音楽家が演奏するときは大ホールが必要です。この施設を使う一人である，ピエール・ブーレーズと話し合った際，彼もまた靴箱型には疑問をもっていると言いました。靴箱型でいくのは止めようと決めました。ところが，私が楕円形を提案したところ，彼は長方形に戻ってほしいと言ってきたのです。

第二の局面で，われわれは，古典的なシンフォニーホールをつくるように依頼され，私は音響技術者の意見に従いました。しかしそれはまったく好きになれませんでした。反響時間を短くするために低い天井の平坦なホールでしたが，空間として好きになれませんでした。私は音響技術者を変えました。私がやりたいと思っていた3つのことがありました。天井の高さを15mにすること。ギャラリー席をつくること。空間構成に円錐形を使うこと。長い反響音を避けるために矩形と円錐を使うという最初の直感

に戻りました。これは長方形と楕円へと展開していきました。ホールの下の階は矩形にしました。側面からの反響音を操作するためです。このために，特別の寸法の一連のパネルを設計し，これは非常にうまく機能しています。

次に，ブーレーズは1階を平坦にしてほしいと頼んできて，これはギャラリー席を設けるという考えに反対するものではないとつけ加えました。1階席が可動なのに対しバルコニー席は固定されています。私にとって楕円の豊かさというのは，異なったジオメトリー，異なった配置の可能性をつくりだすために長い軸線と短い軸線を使えることです。多様な構成ができるのです。1月のオープン以来，座席と舞台構成は

毎週変えられているときます。

**GA**：最初に，この反転した形のコンサートホールを設計されたということですが，この基本的アイディアを外形にも持ち込まれたのですか。

ポルザンパルク：いいえ。これは，パリの高等音楽院にあるペレーの小さなコンサートホールのことを考えているあいだに浮かんだものだったと思います。非常に面白く美しい空間で，その形はとても独特なものです。あのような形のなかに音を部分的にとどめたら面白いだろうと感じました。背の高いホールにすると天井が問題であることは知っていましたので，音をもっと吸収するジオメトリーをもつ形態を探しました。ある仕事に十分長くかかわっていると，時

**Portzamparc:** No, I think this emerged while I was thinking of Perret's little concert hall in Paris—the École Normale de Musique—which is a very interesting and beautiful space. In shape it is quite unique. For the auditorium I felt it would be interesting if the sound could be kept partly within a shape like that. I knew that if I wanted a high hall the ceiling would be a problem, so I looked for a shape whose geometry was more sound-absorbent. Some intuitions can prove fruitful if you work on them long enough. But it wasn't a question of scientific acoustics. If I had started with the acoustic problem, I don't think I would have ended up with this form.

Anyway, we were taking a risk. The acousticians told me the design was inadequate, because we would have to make a large number of additions. We continued with our calculations. The results weren't bad but we kept on working right up to the opening. I came to realize that the musicians themselves would have to learn the acoustics of the place. Concert halls are like musical instruments. They all play differently. When Daniel Barenboim gave a solo concert in January, I was apprehensive, because he tends to play very loud. Some weeks before the concert I placed a piano where he would be playing and

found the echoes were strong. But the concert itself was absolutely magical. Afterwards he told me he loved the hall. For ten minutes before the concert he had listened to the acoustics and modulated his playing in response to the hall. He adapted very quickly: a great musician listens to the entire space, not just the piano.

**GA:** Since this particular project, I know that you have been asked to design several concert halls. You have become a master of concert halls.

**Portzamparc:** I would be prudent with such praise. I took many risks, and of course I wasn't alone. I was encouraged by my acoustician, Yy Ya Ying, and by IRCAM's team of acousticians, who regularly tested and criticized our project. We have been very lucky with the great hall, which seems to have achieved high-quality

sound in a novel form. But We certainly made a few mistakes in parts of the building. There is a lot to say about the Cité de la Musique because there were thousands of problems to solve: a highly complex program, functional questions, the urban context, the events I wanted to unfold inside the building, and the quality of forms and space. In fact, the project became a sort of laboratory for my work. On the one hand the program was highly specific, but on the other, many of my general architectural themes were integrated into the project. But, because I originally conceived of it ten years ago, it is hard for me to discuss today. I am doing other things. I am myself in motion. I don't like to do the same thing twice. So in a way, talking about the Cité de la Musique is like saying good bye to it, because it's past history.

*View from north: dance studio on top*　北より見る：最上階はダンス・スタジオ

に直感が正しいことがあります。しかしそれは科学的音響の問題ではありません。もし音響の問題から始めていたとしたら，この形態にはたどり着けなかったと思います。

いずれにせよ，私たちは危険に賭けたわけです。音響技術者たちは，たくさんのものを付け加えなければならないだろうからこのデザインは適切ではないと僕に言いました。私たちは計算を続けました。結果は悪くありませんでしたが，開館まで手を入れていました。そして，音楽家自身がそのホールの音響を学ぶべきであることに気づきました。コンサートホールは楽器のようなものなので，どれもが違った演奏をするのです。1月にダニエル・バレンボイムが独奏会を開くことになって，私は心配でした。彼の演奏は非常に激しいものとなる傾向がありましたから。演奏会の数週間前，彼が演奏する位置にピアノを置いてみて，やはり反響が強いことを発見しました。しかし演奏会はまったく魔法のようでした。演奏の後で，彼はこのホールが好きだと言ってくれました。演奏の10分前に，音を聴いて，ホールに対応して演奏を調節したのです。彼は素早く対応しました。優れた音楽家はピアノだけでなく，ホール全体を聴くものです。

**GA**：このプロジェクトを完成されてから，コンサートホールの設計をたくさん依頼されてい

ます。コンサートホールの熟達者になられたわけですね。

**ポルザンパルク**：そのような賛辞には慎重にならざるを得ません。多くの危険をかけましたし，そしてもちろん一人でできたことではありません。常に音響をテストしてくれ批評してくれた，音響専門家のイー・ヤー・インやIRCAMのチームに励まされてできたことです。大きなホールで，新しい形を使って，優れた音響を実現できたようにみえることは非常にラッキーだったと思います。しかし建物の小さな部分で多くの失敗をおかしていることも確かです。音楽都市については語ることが多くあるのです。解決しなければならないたくさんの問題がありました

から。複雑なプログラム，機能性，都市的な背景，内側に展開したいと思ったイヴェント，形態と空間の質といったさまざまな問題です。このプロジェクトは私の仕事にとって一種の実験室になりました。一方では，非常に特定の精密なプログラムがあり，一方では，私の一般的な建築テーマが多く入り込んでいます。しかし，これはもともとは10年前に考えたものなので，今，それについて論じることは私には困難です。今，私は別なことをしていますから。私自身，動いているのです。同じことを二度やることは好きではありません。ですから，ある意味で，音楽都市について語ることは，さよならを言うことです。それは過ぎた歴史なのですから。

*View from patio* パティオより見る

*Lounge* ラウンジ

*Lounge* ラウンジ

*Void space* 吹き抜け

*Opening to Boulevard* ブールバールに対して開かれた開口部

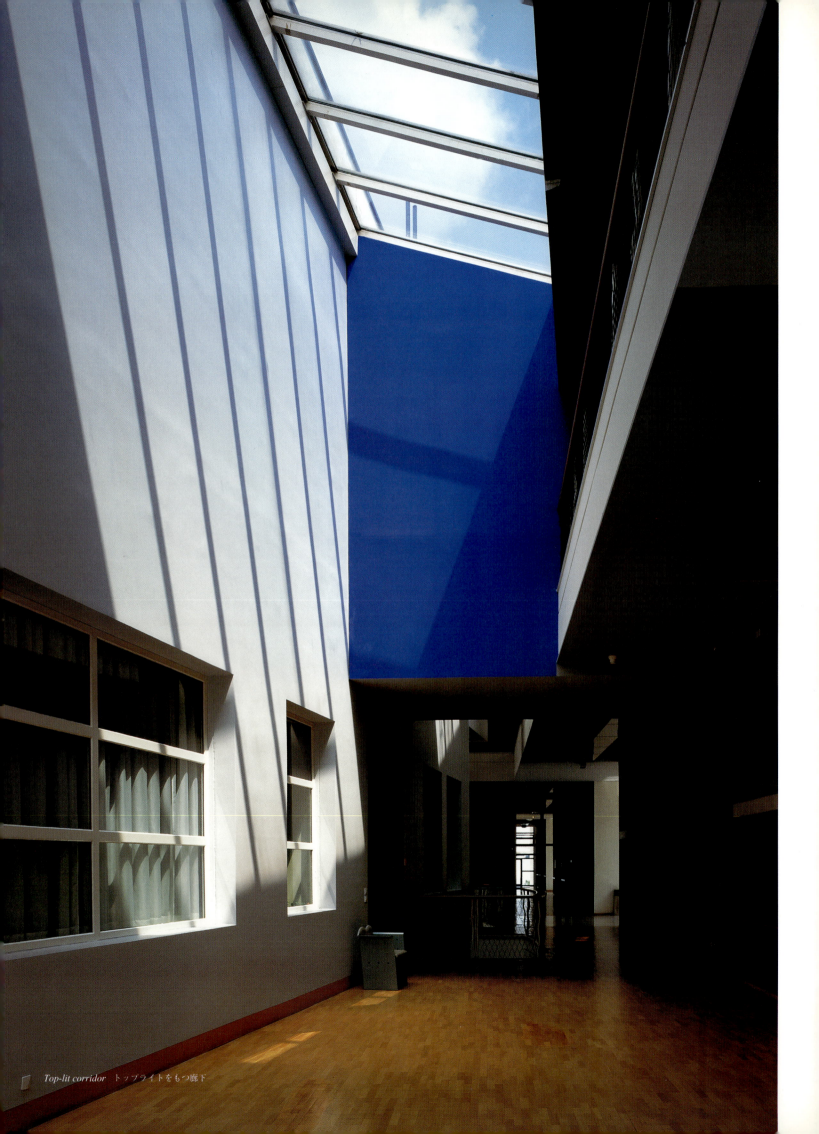

*Top-lit corridor* トップライトをもつ廊下

Small lounge　小ラウンジ

*Music studio* 音楽スタジオ

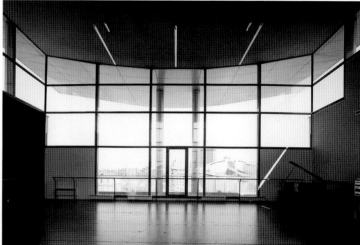

*View toward void space* 吹き抜け方向を見る

*Dance studio* ダンス・スタジオ

*Gymnasium* 体育館

*Music studio* 音楽スタジオ

*Music studio* 音楽スタジオ

*Gymnasium* 体育館

*Study*

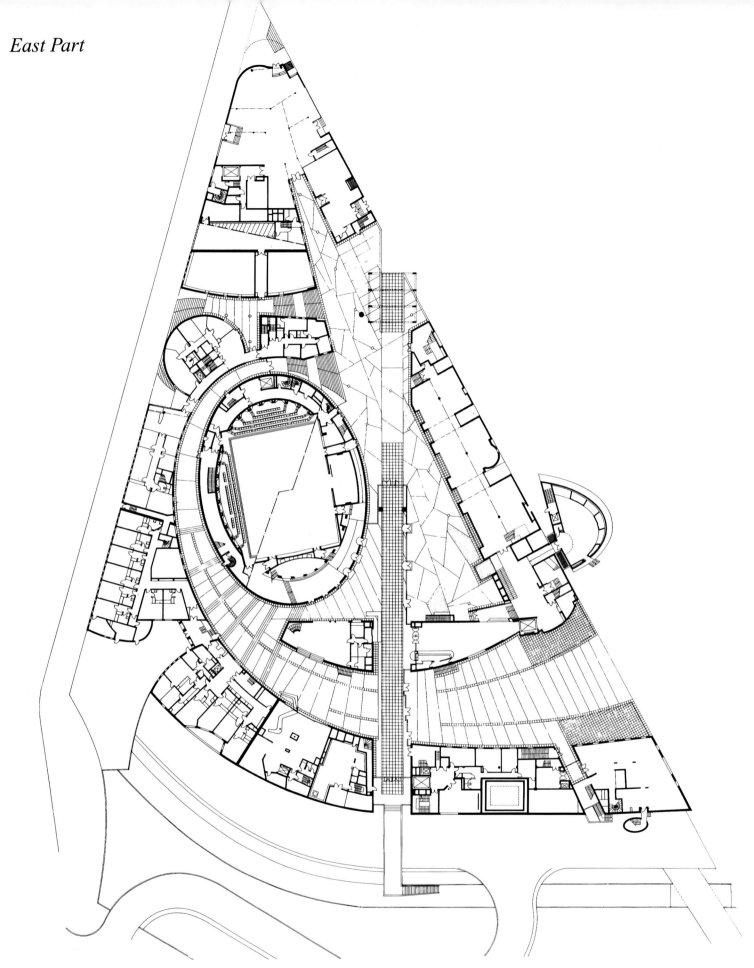

*Ground & first floor plan: public access*

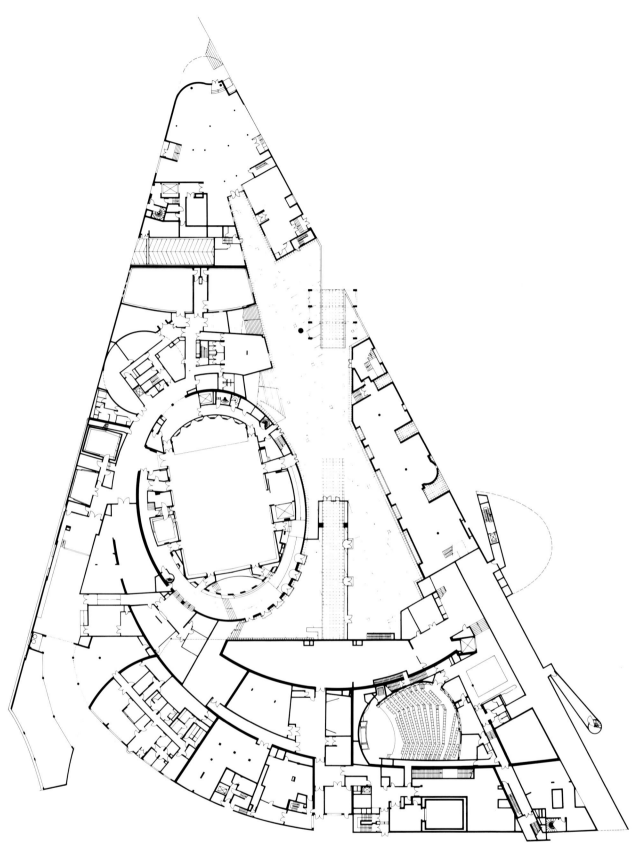

*Ground floor plan*

*Section: concert hall, museum, student accommodation, information center, Café, foyer, rehearsal halls & parking*

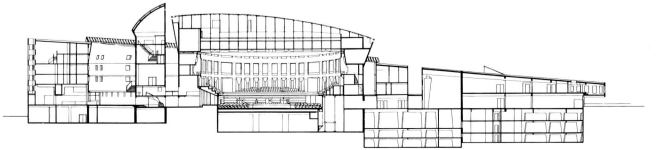

67

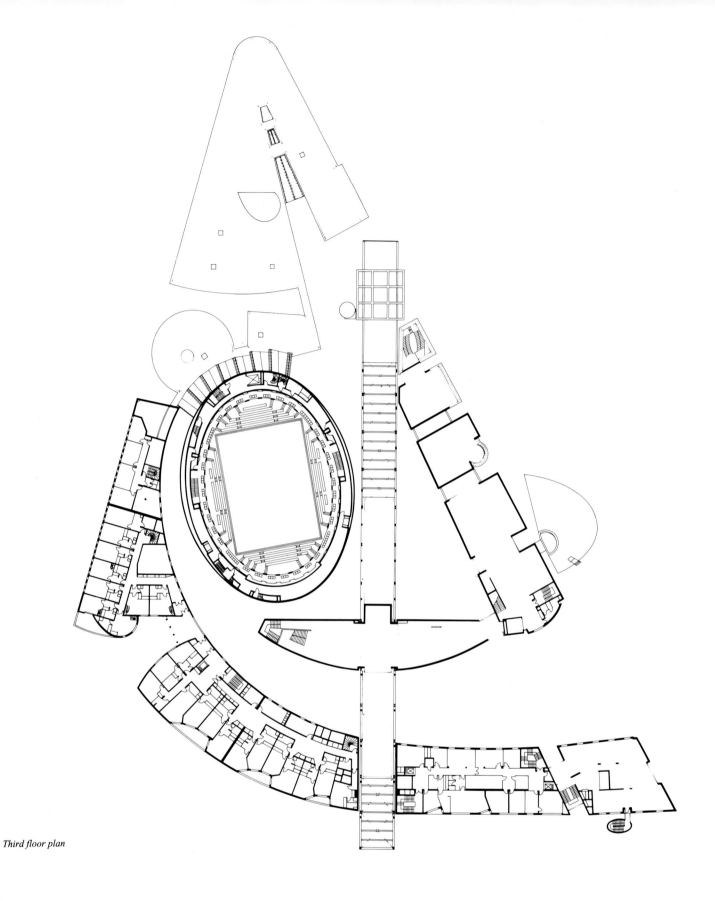

*Third floor plan*

*Section: metal beam, amphitheater, offices, foyer & parking*

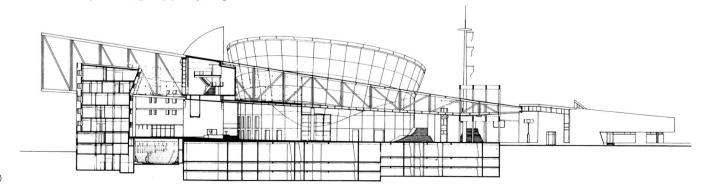

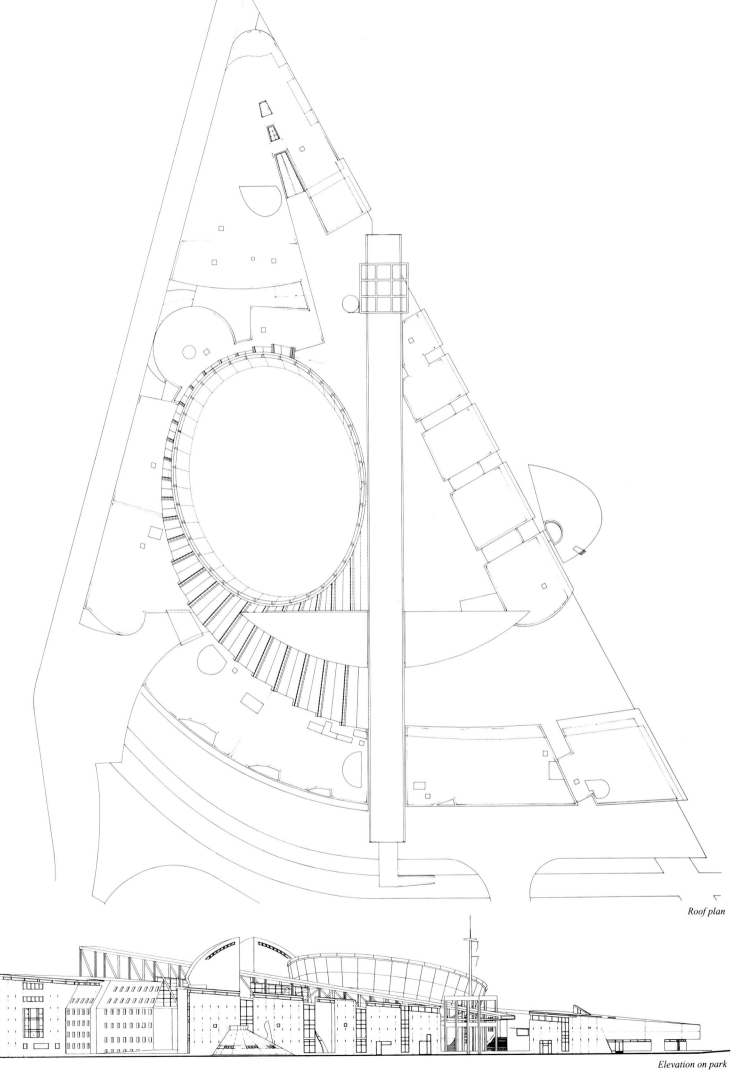

*Roof plan*

*Elevation on park*

71

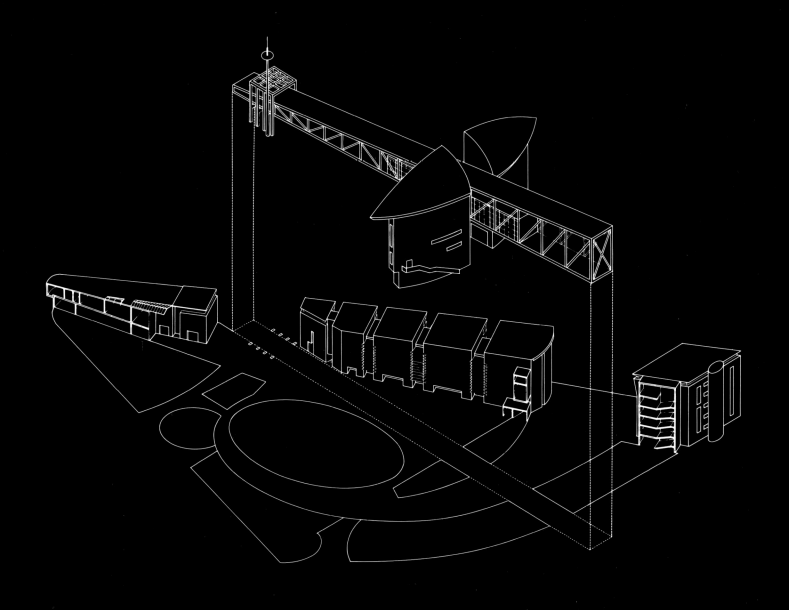

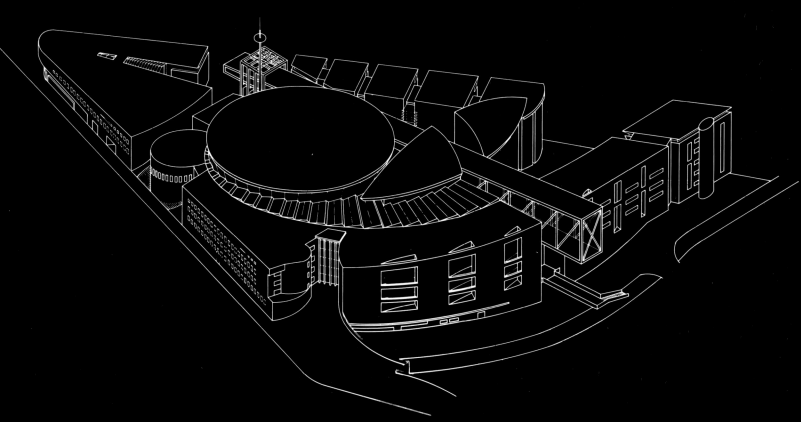

*Axonometric*

*Studies*

*Elevation on Boulevard Périphérique*

*Overall view of southeast* 南東側全景

*Elevation on Boulevard Jean Jaurès*

*View from north* 北より見る

*Overall view from park* 公園より見る

*View toward main entrance* メイン・エントランスを見る

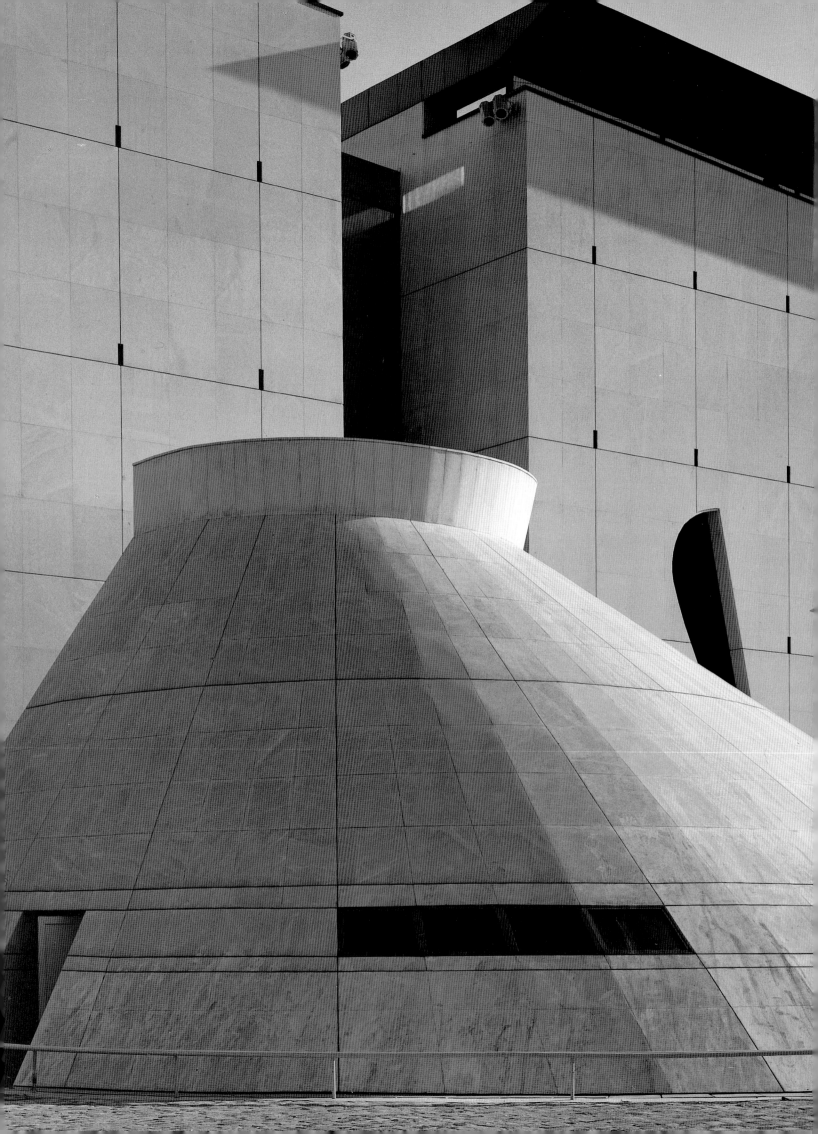

West elevation of museum　ミュージアム西側ファサード

*View from entrance courtyard* エントランスコートより見る

*View toward main entrance*　メイン・エントランスを見る

Entrance hall　エントランス・ホール

Foyer ホワイエ

*Entrance of concert hall* コンサート・ホール入口

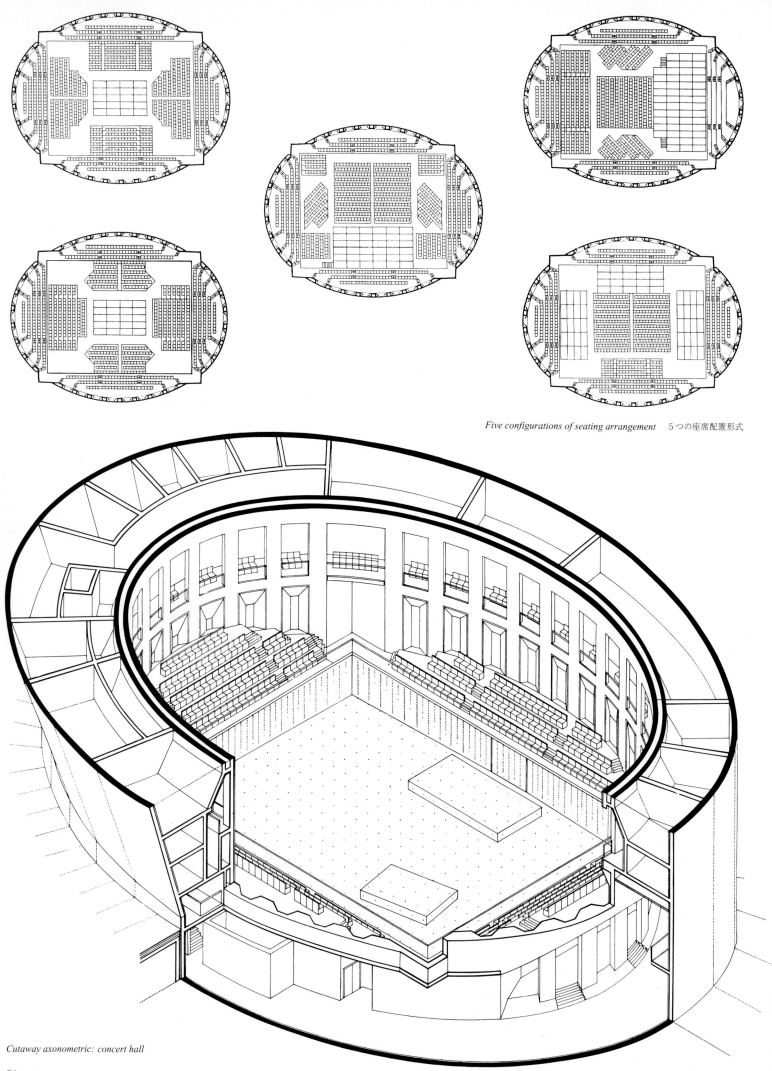

*Five configurations of seating arrangement*　5つの座席配置形式

*Cutaway axonometric: concert hall*

Amphitheater　アンフィシアター

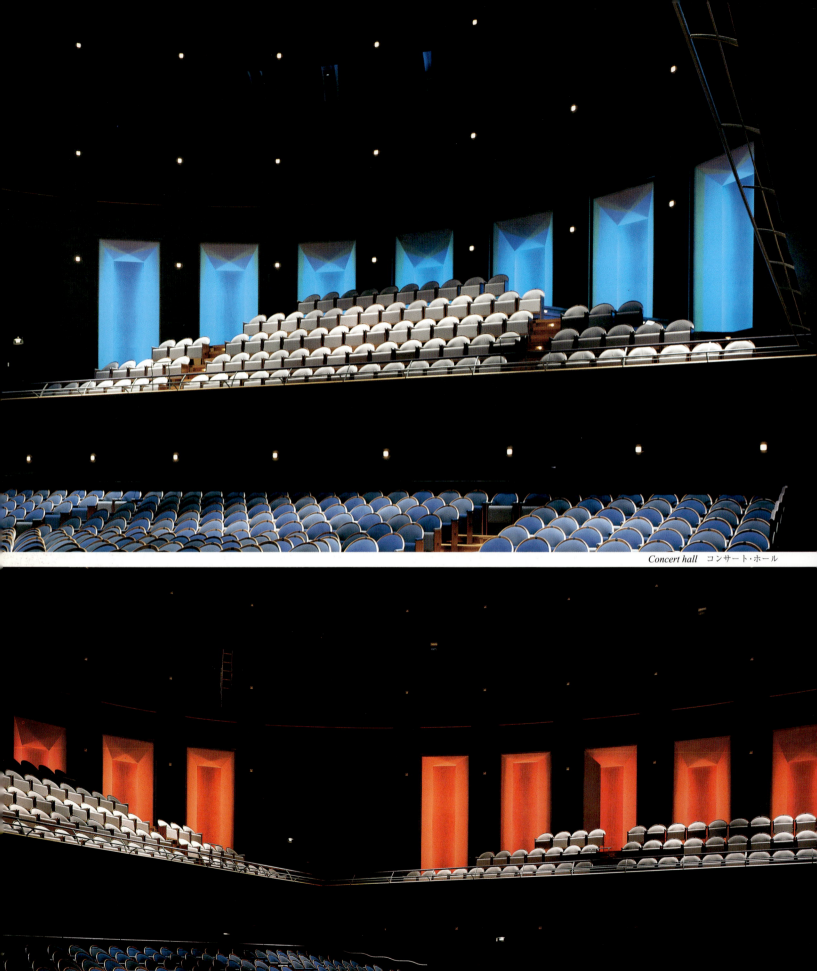

*Concert hall*　コンサート・ホール

*Foyer of amphitheater*　アンフィ・シアターのホワイエ

*Reception of museum*　ミュージアムのレセプション

*Lounge*　ラウンジ

# Rue Nationale, Urban Rehabilitation
## ナスィオナル街計画

Rue Nationale, Paris, France

Client: RIVP   Program: Rehabilitation Palulos 1st and 2nd phase—rehabilitation of social housing units built in the sixties and creation and rearrangement of a garden; Housing—two villa buildings, 19 housing units, shops, parking units; Cultural Center—cultural center and new technology workshops for A.D.A.C., offices, artist's studios   Design and construction period: 1990–93 (1st phase), 1992–94 (2nd phase), 1990–94 (Housing)   1991– (Cultural Center)   Total floor areas: 24,989 m² (1st phase); 65,600 m² (2nd phase)   Building areas: 8,700 m² (Housing); 2,600 m² (Cultural Center)   Engineers: Sodetec, Eurotec (Cultural Center)   Quantity surveyor: Atec (Cultural Center)   Landscaping consultant: Lydye Chauvac (1st phase)   Landscaping: Jardem Environment (1st and 2nd phase)   Metals: S3M (1st phase)   General Contractor: Sicra

*View of after rehabilitation*   改修後

*Study*

*View of rue Nationale before rehabilitation* 改修以前のナスィオナル街

*Under construction* 工事中

*View from garden* 庭より見る

**GA:** What is the nature of this project? And what were your goals?

**Portzamparc:** The Place Nationale is not far from the Hautes Formes which I built twenty years ago. I was asked to rehabilitate four buildings: two large slab blocks and two small ones. For me the project was an interesting experiment in transforming a neighborhood. I often talk about what I call the Three Ages of the City. Obviously in all our cities, we have contradictory areas. Some are based on Age 1, with geometries and forms on the classical Greek, Roman or medieval models and extending all the way to Baroque and neoclassical architecture. Age 2 cities are the modernist cities comprising upon huge slab blocks and towers. Here in Paris, we have a nineteenth century network which developed out of the earlier villages. The house and garden were gradually replaced by multistory buildings. The older buildings were rather poor in quality and few have survived in the thirteenth neighborhood. The street layout was kept and housing blocks were built in the Age 2 manner. We analyzed this.

**GA:** So you were trying to resolve this conflict with your own urban ideas?

**Portzamparc:** Yes, I decided to try to give new meaning to the street fronts. The building facing the Place Nationale was too big, and cast too much shadow on the areas around it, so I decided to replace it entirely. Its inhabitants have been relocated in two villa-buildings which I positioned along the street. These mediate between the scale of the street and the huge housing blocks behind them. I think this introduces some interesting relationships. I decided that these pavilions and the renovated slabs could create the envelope for a semi-private garden, making the whole complex like a village. You now have a clear demarcation between private and public spaces, which did not exist before. I also decided to make openings in the slab blocks by taking out some studios at ground level. This opened the buildings up to the garden and the west and marked the entrance while preserving the scale of the "village." It also let in more light. We then added covered passageways leading from the street to the main slab blocks to give shelter from the rain. The entrance to the village is located between the two villa buildings.

**GA:** What did you do to the slabs themselves?

**Portzamparc:** We did quite a lot. We renovated the interiors, altered the windows to enhance privacy, and changed the balconies. I swept off the vertical lines, which weren't doing anything. These interventions completely altered the exteriors and the way they are used today. The result is something perhaps a little quieter. We equipped the smaller slab block with large balconies with access through a French window. One morning people discovered they had a new door and a new large space overlooking the garden. We changed the window trimmings to aluminum and the outside covering to fiber cement and metal. The building appears completely new and it's usefulness has been greatly improved.

**GA:** What's the current situation?

**Portzamparc:** We are finishing work on the third slab—the longest—which is positioned along the street. We are trying to create squares along the street to welcome people as they enter. These are slightly set back from the street, with planted areas.

*Newly built villas* 新築のヴィッラ

**GA**：どのような性格のプロジェクトであり，また，何を目標とされたのですか。

**ポルザンパルク**：プラス・ナスィオナルは20年前に私が建てたオート・フォルムからあまり離れていません。大きなスラブ2つと小さなスラブが2つ，計4つの建物の改修を頼まれたのです。このプロジェクトは，ある地区をどのように変化させることができるかという，私にとって興味深い実験でした。ご存知の通り，私はよく都市の3つの時代と呼んでいるものについて話すのですが，明らかに，すべての都市には矛盾する要素が混在する地域があります。いくつかの都市は時代1に属します。古典ギリシアやローマ，あるいは中世それからバロック，新古典へとつながってゆくジオメトリーや形態で構成されています。時代2は巨大なスラブ・ブロックやタワーで構成されたモダニストの都市です。パリには村から発展した19世紀の都市のネットワークが存在しています。家や庭は徐々に多層の建物に置き換わってきました。古い建物はかなり質が悪く，この13番地にはあまり残っていません。街路のレイアウトはそのまま残され，集合住宅は時代2の方法で建てられてきました。私たちはこれを分析しました。

**GA**：その矛盾を都市に対する自論で解決なさろうということですね。

**ポルザンパルク**：ええ，街路に面する側に新しい意味をつくりだそうと決心しました。ナスィオナル広場に面する建物はあまりにも大きすぎるため，周囲を影にしていますので，全体を取り替えることにしました。その建物の住民には通り沿いに建てた2つのヴィラタイプの建物に移動してもらいます。これらの建物は街路のもつスケールとその背後の巨大なハウジングとの間の一種の調停者の役割を果たします。何か面白い関係が生まれるのではないかと思ったのです。これらのヴィラと改修されるスラブ型の建物はセミプライベートな庭の囲みをつくりだせるはずで，それによって，全体が村のようになると考えました。以前にはなかったプライベートとパブリックな場との境界がはっきりするわけです。またスラブ・タイプの建物は1階にあったスタジオをいくつか取り去り，開口をとることにしました。これによって建物全体は庭と西に向けて開放され，"村"のスケールを維持しながらエントランスには存在感が生まれますし，光も前より豊かに差し込みます。道路から主要なスラブ・ブロックを結んで，雨をしのげる屋根付きの通路を付けました。この村へのエントランスは2つのヴィラの間にあります。

**GA**：スラブ・タイプの建物にはどのような改修をされたのですか。

**ポルザンパルク**：いろいろとやりました。インテリアを改造し，プライバシーを強調するために窓を取り替え，バルコニーも変え，何の意味もない垂直の線を消去しました。この作業で使い方も，全体の外壁の構成も完全に変わりました。以前よりおとなしいものになったかもしれません。小さい方のスラブにはフランス窓から出入りできる大きなバルコニーをつけました。ある朝，住民は，新しいドアと庭を見晴らす新しい広い空間があることに気がつくのです。窓枠をアルミ製のものにし，外壁はメタルと繊維セメントにしました。建物の外観は完全に一新され，ずっと使いやすいものになりました。

**GA**：今はどのような状況なのですか。

**ポルザンパルク**：道路に沿った，一番長い3つ目の建物の仕上げ中です。道沿いに，ここに来る人々を歓迎するような広場をつくろうとしています。そこは植栽した部分だけ道路からは少し後退させています。

*Study: building for technical amenities*

*View of after rehabilitation* 改修後

*Entrance*　エントランス

*Entrance hall*　エントランス・ホール

*Entrance hall*　エントランス・ホール

*View from rue Nationale*　ナスィオナル街より見る

*View from garden*　庭より見る

# Apartment Buildings PL1, ZAC Bercy
## ベルシーの都市再生計画・アパートPL1

Supervisor: SEMAEST (Architecte ZAC: J.P. Buffi)   Client: C.A.R.C.D.
Program: 67 housing units, 5 commercial spaces, 118 parking units
Design and construction period: 1991–94   Structural system: reinforced concrete
Building area: 12,861 m²   General contractor: Sopac

ZAC Bercy, Paris, France

**GA:** This is part of a masterplan by Jean-Pierre Buffi, a housing project in the wake of the Hautes Formes. Tell me about your design strategy.

**Portzamparc:** I was given a building and two objects. The masterplan organized the work of a dozen quite dissimilar projects on a long park-front, creating a series of urban blocks. The brief stipulated that I incorporate balconies at certain heights to maintain unity. I thought this had potential but that the block itself was a little bit too closed. As I often mention, analysis of the block is central to my work. In both architectural and town-planning terms, we need to open up the city block and reintroduce the street. The site in question was more or less a closed block, but there were some openings so I thought it might be the beginning of something. The closed block, with buildings stuck together in the traditional manner, was fitting in the nineteenth century. But I have constantly criticized the reversion back to this type of block. It just won't work today, for several reasons.

The architecture might be passable, but the closed block disallows the use of light and volumes which is the culture of architecture today. The age when the rhetoric of the facade was codified is over and gone. That was the traditional city. In contemporary architecture, we have to recognize that the object is the paradigm. Of course, this object has then to adapt to urban situations, but it does not have to be systematically closed off.

**GA:** How did the scheme come together?

**Portzamparc:** First I worked on the small objects, shaping them so that they could be seen from the park. Then I treated the roof so that more light would enter the building, and the gardens so that the trees would be in front of the windows. I had great difficulty with this building since so much of it was in shadow. I felt that the courtyard was a bit too cramped and this posed another problem. I didn't want to close off the courtyard. At this point the project was stopped for a year because there were complications with a law

against destroying any trees. This was fortunate for me. The client was losing money, so I proposed we keep the trees by opening up a little more space. The site became more the type of urban situation I prefer. We kept the trees and a sense of openness from the ground and upper floors.

**GA:** I notice that there are quite a lot of double-height rooms. Were these part of the program?

**Portzamparc:** A certain floor area was required. I was working with an interesting and highly specific scenario here. In some places I designed tall sitting rooms like small-scale duplexes. I thought everybody should have a balcony, even those living on floors between the established balcony lines. But this proved impossible, so my solution was to have balconies for certain units and gardens for the others. I put the living rooms on the corners because then they would have long views. This works very well. Obviously if I had kept to the original brief, the views would have been

*Section*

more restricted. The trees and the sunlight in front of the living rooms make you forget you are on the north side. It creates an agreeable atmosphere that wasn't very favorable in the first place. In other parts I used glass bay windows and a balcony. By creating these different types of rooms I think I have managed to achieve some interesting spaces despite the dense situation.

**GA:** You also opened up the corners.

**Portzamparc:** These window-openings lend a degree of transparency and a sense of lightness to the corners. I created two different situations. When you have the large balcony you have bay windows, and when you have a veranda you have corner windows. Some of the apartments are more like the traditional type of duplex, with both high and low parts in the living areas. The little tower in the courtyard lends a sense of playfulness. I think it works better than the other courtyards which are more closed off. This is the important contribution here. It was just by chance that the project became an interesting experiment for my theory of the open block, to test my theory that it is possible to have achieve high-density and have light and effective views. Some of the views might not be so wide but they can be effective if they are well made. This is a street situation and so you need long views. Ever since the Hautes Formes I have always said we need short and long views in our cityscapes, creating intimacy and opening up vistas. Not just the long-distance views of the Modernists, and not just the intimacy and compactness of the beautiful old city, but both.

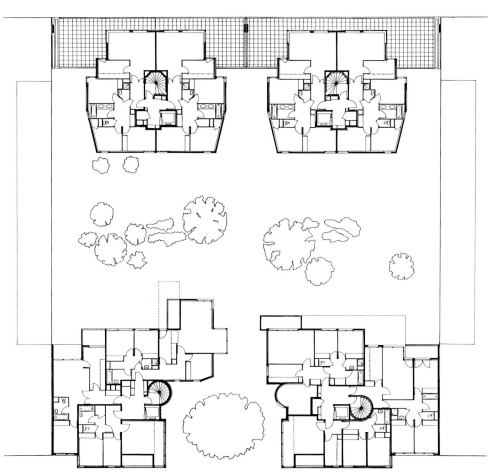

*Typical floor plan*

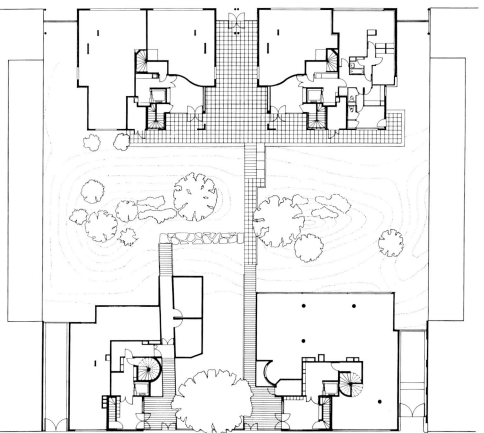

*Section*

*Ground floor plan*

*Overall view from park on south* 南側公園からの全景

*Roof*　最上部

*Courtyard*　中庭

**GA**：マスタープランはジャン=ピエール・ビュッフィによるもので，オート・フォルムに続くハウジング・プロジェクトですね。どのようなデザイン上のストラテジーをとられたのですか。

**ポルザンパルク**：私は建物を一つとオブジェを2つ頼まれました。マスタープランは，長く続く公園に面して1ダースの全く異なった形のハウジングを建て，一連の都市ブロックを構成しようというものです。設計要綱には，統一性を保持するために，特定のバルコニーを一定の高さで使うことが明記されていました。バルコニーはうまく使える可能性がありますが，ブロックは閉鎖的すぎると思いました。よく言っていることですが，都市ブロックの分析は，私の仕事の中心にあるものです。建築においても，都市計画においても，都市ブロックを開き，街路を再び導入することが必要なのです。この敷地は多かれ少なかれ閉鎖的なブロックです。しかし，所々にオープンな部分もあるのでここが何かの出発点になるのではないかと思いました。建物が一団となった，伝統的な手法である閉鎖的なブロックは，19世紀には適合していたわけです。しかし，私はこのようなタイプのブロックに戻ろうとする動きを常に批判してきました。いくつかの理由から，そうしたものは今日うまく機能しないのです。建物は通り抜けできるかもしれませんが，現代建築の文化となっている，ヴォリュームを操作したり光を使うことを許容しません。ファサードのレトリックが体系化されているような時代は過ぎ去ったのです。それは伝統的な都市のものでした。現代建築ではオブジェがパラダイムであることを認識しなければなりません。もちろん，このオブジェはその都市状況に適応させなければなりませんが，システマティックに閉鎖すべきではありません。

**GA**：それでどのようになされたのですか。

**ポルザンパルク**：小さなオブジェから始め，公園から見えるような形にしました。次によく光が入るような形に屋根をデザインし，窓の前に木立がくるように庭を構成しました。大部分が影になるため，この建物の設計は非常に難しいものでした。中庭が少し狭苦しすぎるような気がしていましたが，これが別の問題になりました。閉鎖的な中庭をつくる気はなかったのです。この時点でプロジェクトは1年間中断しました。というのは木を伐採してはならないという法律のため事態が複雑化したからです。この一時中断は私にとっては幸運でした。この中断によりオーナーは損失を受けつつあったので，私は敷地にもう少し空き地をとることで，木を残すことができると提案しました。敷地は前より開放的になり，私にとってずっと好ましいタイプの都市用地になりました。木立を残し，1階や上階には解放感が生まれたわけです。

**GA**：2層吹抜けの部屋が数多くあることに気づいたのですが，これもプログラムの一部だったのですか。

**ポルザンパルク**：ある程度の床面積が求められていました。ここでは，面白く，特別なシナリオに沿って設計しました。何カ所かで，私は天井の高い，小型のデュプレックスのような居間をつくりました。どのユニットにもバルコニーを付けるべきだと思ったのです。既定のバルコニーの高さの中間に位置するこれらの居間にもですね。しかし，それはできませんでした。そこで私の解決案は，バルコニー付きユニットと庭付きユニットに分けることでした。リビングルームはコーナーに位置するようにしました。そうすることで景色が遠くまで見えるからです。これはとても上手くゆきました。もし，私が元々の設計要綱を守っていたとしたら，眺めはこれほど広々としたものにはならなかったでしょう。眺めはもっと限定されたものになったこ

とは明らかです。居間の前の木立や日差しは，この部屋が北向きであることを忘れさせ，最初は感心したものではなかった雰囲気を快いものにしています。他の部分にはガラス張りの出窓やバルコニーを使いました。違った種類の部屋をつくることによって，密度が高いという条件にもかかわらず，面白い空間をつくることができたのだと思います。

**GA**：また，コーナーを大きく開いていますね。

**ポルザンパルク**：この窓の開口は，一種の透明感と軽やかさをコーナーに与えています。私は2つのケースを設定しました。広いバルコニーがついているユニットには出窓，ベランダがある場合にはコーナーウインドウをつけることにしたのです。何戸かのアパートは，リビングルームに高低差のある伝統的なデュプレックス・タイプに似た構成にしています。中庭にある小さな塔は陽気な雰囲気をつくりだしています。この中庭は，他の閉鎖的な中庭よりもうまく機能していますし，ここでは重要な役割を果たしています。このプロジェクトが私のオープンブロック説，高密度であっても光や良い眺めを取り入れられるという理論を実証する良い機会になったのは全くの偶然です。眺めがあまり広くとれない場所も確かにあります。しかし，景観構成を工夫することで小さな眺望も効果的なものにすることができます。ここは通りに面した敷地なので奥行きのある眺めが必要となってきます。オート・フォルム以来，景観の中に奥行きの深いものと浅いものを組み合わせることが必要であると主張してきました。つまり親密さと広がりのある解放感を組み合わせることが必要だと思うのです。モダニストの都市の奥行きのある眺めだけでも，古い都市の暖かく小さな美しい眺めだけでもなく，両方が必要なのです。

*Interior of unit*　アパート内部

*Interior of unit*　アパート内部

*balcony*　バルコニー

# Crédit Lyonnais Tower
## クレディ・リヨネ・タワー

Supervisor: Euralille   Euralille Urban Design: Rem Koolhaas   Client: Ferinel Industries—Groupe George V for the Crédit Lyonnais   Program: offices Design and construction period: 1991–95   Structural system: reinforced concrete Area: 17,000 m²   Engineers: S.E.E.R. (structure), C.E.E.F. (exterior cladding), Serete (fluids)   Contractors: Caroni—Groupe C.B.C. (structure), Harmon C.F.E.M. (exterior cladding)

Lille, France

*Overall view*   全景

*Elevation*

*Elevation*

*Section*

*North elevation*

*North-east elevation: competition phase*

GA: This tower project for Euralille was being designed by Richard Rogers before they asked you to design it, even though you hadn't really built a tower before. How did you become involved?

Portzamparc: It's true that I had never designed a tower before. When I was asked by Rem Koolhaas to do some work on the Euralille projects, I joked to Rem that he wanted to employ me as a foil, a comic actor in a tragedy—or vice versa!

The client said the main volume of the original proposal was too big, more than they could afford. It gave a view of the rails but not of the city. They wanted views of the existing city. The building also had to be a bridge, since it formed the center of the station. They said that the mass was too heavy and the surface area too great. They asked if I could reduce the overall volume and design something different. Rem said I could use any shape I wanted as long as it reached a height of 100 meters and included a bridge. I tried out different shapes, with many variants. Then slowly I came up with the idea of using one leg as part of the tower. The legs are very thin. I essentially put the weight on one point and used the bridge as a truss to maintain stability. I ended up with a basic L-shape. Then I opened it up so that more offices would have views of the city. I also organized the shape to let more light into certain areas.

GA: Was structure an important consideration for you when you were looking for design solutions?

Portzamparc: Definitely. For example, initially I had interior beams which used the whole geometry of the shape, but then they asked me to get rid of everything inside. So we finally placed strong beams supporting the floors in all the technical areas. It's an enormous structure—one hundred meters across. We had to work a lot on the structure and on the glazing systems. One part is curtain wall, facing the city. This is a limit that lets more light into the recessed parts of the offices. It is particularly thin. I wanted the other areas to be open and so I used windows. This brought in light from above. I think it strikes a good balance between inside protection and the need to have light and views. I think if it was completely open in this situation you would feel exposed—you would no longer have an inside, as if you were behind a collapsing wall, so to speak.

GA: Could you tell us more about your treatment of the exterior?

Portzamparc: I enjoyed working with the metal panels. The panels are gray-green and the glass is also slightly green. When clouds go by there is an alternation between the reflecting glass and the non-reflecting steel. The green of the surfaces plays off against the blue gray of the sky. It's a balance l tried to add to the presence of the tower.

GA: How did the other projects in Euralille affect your design choices? Were you aware of the other designs? Or were you more interested in the existing context?

Portzamparc: I didn't really look at the surroundings for clues. I knew the general context, but I wasn't looking for anything in particular. Only afterwards did I realize that Jean Nouvel's Shopping Mall had incorporated an inclined angle and that my project and his were playing each other off. I didn't have any particular contextual organization in mind. I concentrated on program, stability, economy, and form. But in the end we found this interplay between oblique lines. It's a chance event, but one I have come to appreciate.

---

GA：ユーラリールのタワー・プロジェクトは，あなたが依頼される前に，リチャード・ロジャース氏が既に設計されていたものですね。まだタワーらしいタワーのご経験は無かったわけですが，どのようにして，これを引き受けることになったのでしょう。

ポルザンパルク：確かに，それまでにタワーを設計したことはありませんでした。レム・コールハースにユーラリールのプロジェクトの仕事を頼まれたとき，レムに，悲劇の中の喜劇役者あるいはその逆のように引き立て役として僕を雇おうというのではないかい，と冗談に言ったものです。

クライアントの話では，最初の提案は主要部のヴォリュームがあまりに大きく受け入れ不可能であり，また，そこからは鉄道方向は望めても，市街への展望がないということでした。彼らはリール市街が望めるようにしてほしかったのです。建物は駅の中心に位置するため，ブリッジの役割を果たす必要もありました。つまり提示案のマスが重すぎ，表面積が広すぎるので，全体のヴォリュームを圧縮して，何か違ったものを設計してほしいということでした。レムから，高さが100mあり，ブリッジがあれば，好きな形にしてよいと言われました。私は異なった形態とそのヴァリエーションを検討しました。そして徐々にタワーの一部を一本脚とするという考えに至ったのです。この脚の厚みはとても薄いので，主に一点に重心を集め，ブリッジを安定性確保のためのトラスとして使うことにしました。こうしてこの基本となっているL字型にたどり着いたのです。次に，より多くのオフィスが市内に向けての眺望を持てるようにタワーを開いていきました。いくつかの場所ではさらに陽光が差し込むように構成しました。

GA：デザインを探していらしたとき，構造は重要な要素だったのでしょうか。

ポルザンパルク：その通りです。たとえば，最初私は形態の全ジオメトリーに利用する梁を室内に渡していたのですが，クライアントから内部からはすべてを撤去してほしいと言われました。そこで最終的にはすべてのテクニカルエリアに床を支える強い梁を設置することにしました。奥行，幅とも100mという巨大な建物です。構造とガラス面の取り付けシステムの設計には時間がかかりました。壁面の一部は市内に面するカーテンウォールです。オフィスの奥にまで光をより多く差し込ませるためには，これが限界でした。カーテンウォールのこの部分はとても薄くしてあります。他の部分は開放的にしたかったので窓を使いました。これは上方から光を取り入れます。このことが室内に保護されているという感覚と光や眺めを必要とすることの間のバランスを程良く保っていると思うのです。この状況で，これ以上開放的であったとすると，むき出しにされているようで，いわば壊れた壁の裏にいるようで，もはや室内にいるとは感じられなくなったでしょう。

GA：外観についてはいかがでしょう。

ポルザンパルク：メタリック・パネルを使うのを楽しみました。パネルは灰緑色で，ガラスも少し緑を帯びています。雲がその面を横切ると，反射ガラスとマットなスチール面の間を交互に動いていくことになります。表面の灰緑色は空の青灰色から分かれて揺らめくのです。これがこのタワーの存在感に私が与えようと思った一つのバランスなのです。

GA：ユーラリールにおける他のプロジェクトは設計にどのような影響を与えましたか。他のデザインを意識したのでしょうか。それともどちらかといえば，その場のコンテクストの方に関心をもたれたのですか。

ポルザンパルク：糸口をつかむために周りの環境に特に目を向けることはしませんでした。全般的な状況については知っていましたが，そこから何かを探すことはしていません。後からジャン・ヌヴェルのショッピング・モールが斜めの角度を組み入れていて，私と彼のプロジェクトが互いに牽制しあうものであることに気がついたのです。私は特定のコンテクスチュアルな構成は頭になく，プログラム，安定性，経済性，形態について集中して考えました。しかし最後に，これらの斜線による相互作用に気が付いたのです。これは偶然に起きたことでしたが，私は満足しています。

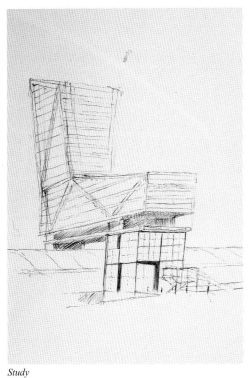

*Study*

*Site plan*

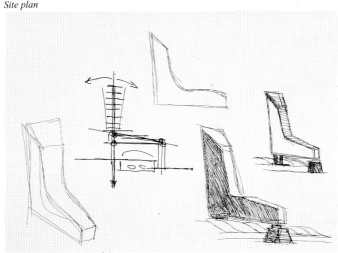

*Study*

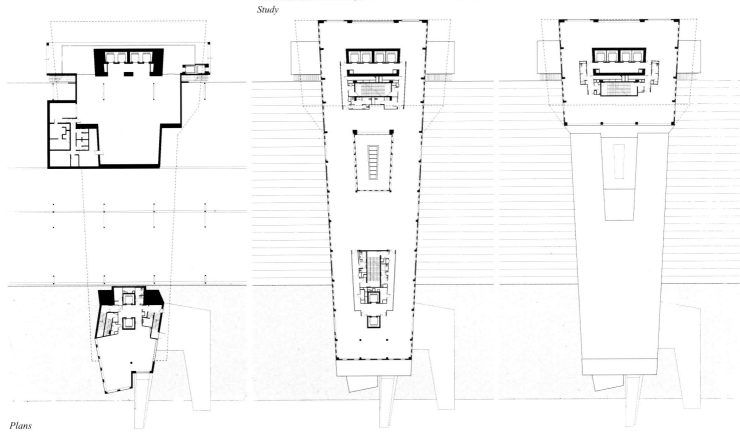

*Plans*

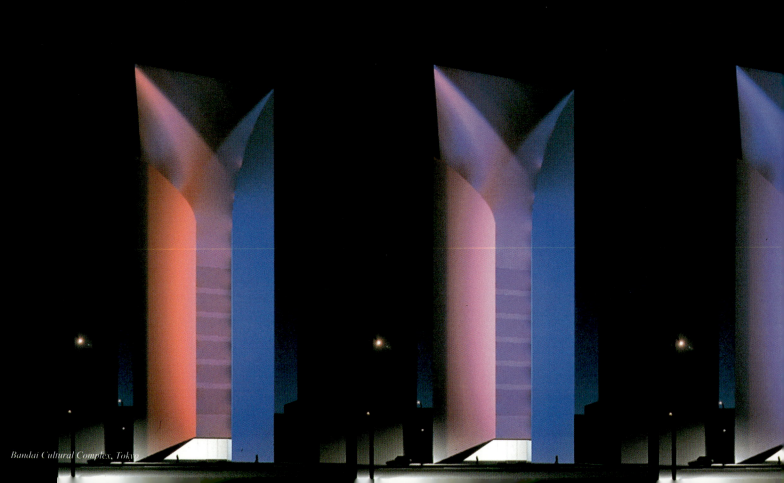

*Bandai Cultural Complex, Tokyo*

# PROJECTS

# Nara International Convention Hall
## 奈良国際会議場

Client: City of Nara   Program: a complex including 2,000-seat concert and convention hall, a 500-seat concert hall, a 100-seat multipurpose hall   Design year: competition in 1992   Structural system: reinforced concrete

Nara, Japan

**Portzamparc:** My work on this project has shifted between the idea to make one structure and several structures. I made a sketch with one and a sketch with several. Using several has been more or less my background. You know I often use fragmented forms. But in general, I want to escape my past and try to change, so this time I tried to design a single structure.

**GA:** So initially you had one form.

**Portzamparc:** Yes. In my first sketches I tried to unify. I related the building to its context in Nara. I was impressed by the beauty of the city center: the grid and the position of the temples, their scale. I thought this new important building could be a modern way to relate to the grid and to the setting of the temples, so I thought it would be good to extend the streets into the geometry of the grid.

I worked on the program as if there were three distinct programs with something which could bring them together—the services and a garden with water in front. The bridge at the entrance is in the right place underneath the hall, and you have the garden surrounded by a cloister. In a way, the project reflects my fascination with Japanese culture.

**GA:** But not aesthetically.

**Portzamparc:** No. It's more topological, the possibility of creating some very remarkable simple spaces close together but distinct from each other. Spaces within spaces. The idea is not just Japanese; such a tradition exists in Europe also. The relationship in between architecture and non-architecture, inside and outside, architecture, and nature: all these things are strong in Japan.

**GA:** Yes. But sort of diluted, without a particular division between inside and outside.

**Portzamparc:** At the same time you have a continuity between inside and outside, but you also have the building which is on

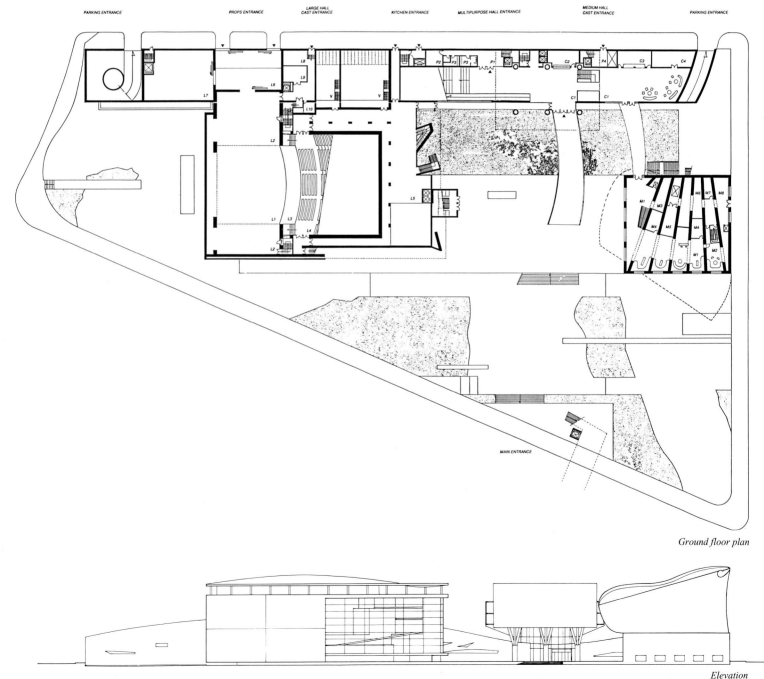

PARKING ENTRANCE   PROPS ENTRANCE   LARGE HALL CAST ENTRANCE   KITCHEN ENTRANCE   MULTIPURPOSE HALL ENTRANCE   MEDIUM HALL CAST ENTRANCE   PARKING ENTRANCE

MAIN ENTRANCE

*Ground floor plan*

*Elevation*

**ポルザンパルク**：このプロジェクトでは，一つの棟にするか，いくつかの棟で構成するかで気持ちが揺れました。1棟の案と数棟による案のスケッチを描きました。いくつかの棟を使うというのは多かれ少なかれ私のバックグラウンドになっています。断片化させた形態をよく使うのはご存知でしょう。しかし，だいたい私は自分の過去から逃げ，変化したいと思っているので，今回は単体の建物をデザインしてみようとしました。

**GA**：最初の段階では一つの形を提起されましたね。

**ポルザンパルク**：ええ。最初のスケッチでは一つにまとめてみました。建物を奈良というコンテクストにつなげたのです。奈良の中心部の美しさ，その町割のグリッド，寺院の位置とスケール感に打たれましたので，この新しい重要な建物は，現代的方法でこのグリッドと寺院配置に関係づけることができるはずだと思いました。それで，敷地内に構成される道をこのグリッドの中へと伸ばしていったら良いのではないかと考えたのです。

サーヴィス・エリアや前面の池のある庭園によって一つにまとまる，3つのプログラムがあるということを想定して設計することにしました。入口にあるブリッジはホールの真下にあり，そして回廊に囲まれた庭があります。ある意味で，このプロジェクトには日本文化に私が魅了されたことが反映されています。

**GA**：しかし美意識的な面にではありませんね。

**ポルザンパルク**：違います。もっとトポロジカルなものです。いくつかの非常に独特で単純な場所を密接して，しかしお互いに分離したものとしてつくりだす可能性についてです。空間のなかの空間といいますか。これは単に日本的というものではありません。こうした伝統はヨーロッパにも存在しています。建築と非建築的なもの，内部と外部，建築と自然，こうしたものの間の関係。それが日本では強いのです。

**GA**：そうですね。しかし，内部と外部の間には特別の分割のない，一種希薄なものです。

**ポルザンパルク**：同時に，内部と外部の連続性があるわけです。しかし脚や基部の上に乗って，庭や池から分離した建物があります——自然のエレメントと人がつくった物との間に対話があり，これが日本ではとても面白いのです。それはイギリスの庭園の伝統のなかにもありますが，イタリアやフランスにはないものです。イタリアやフランスの伝統では，庭園は建築の一部であり，しかし，その線は無限に伸びていきます。禅の庭のエレメントの対話，自然との修辞的対立のなかに存在する建築概念が私は気に入っています。これは18世紀の自然に対する浪漫的な態度に広がっているもので，ルドゥーやドイツ新古典主義のシンケルにとって重要なものとなりました。

**GA**：建物そのものについてはどうなのでしょう。何を実現されようとしたのですか。

**ポルザンパルク**：私は主に2つの空間について考えました。一つは大きなコンサート兼会議場

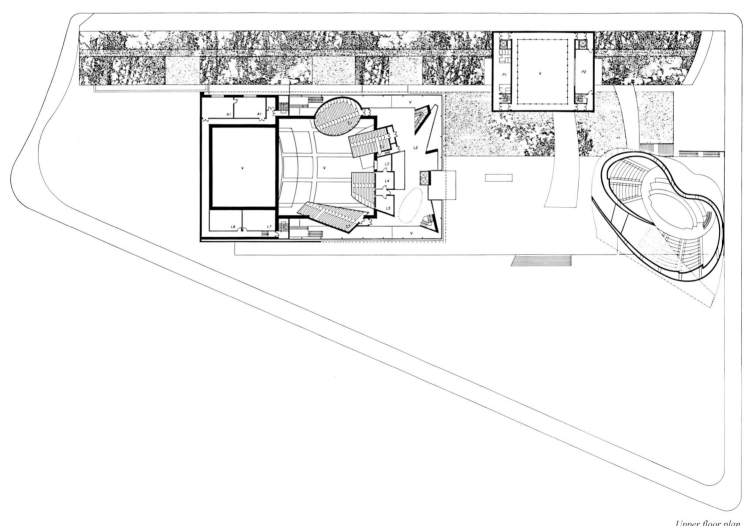

*Upper floor plan*

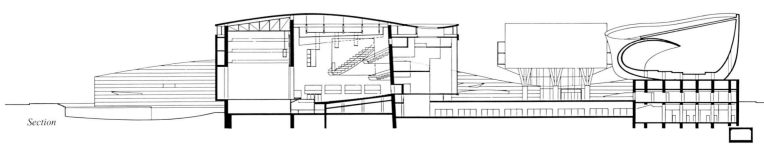

*Section*

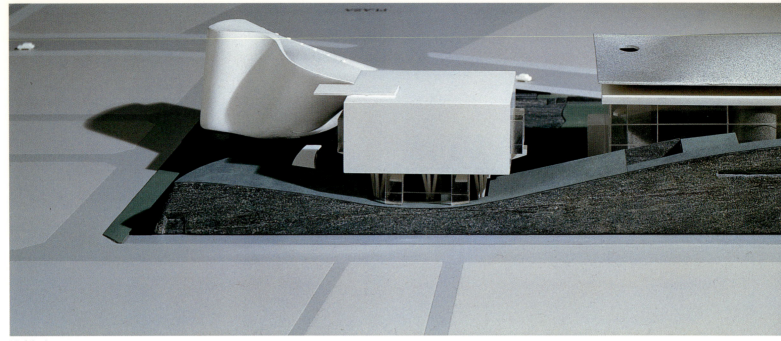

*Model: elevation on street*

*CG: large concert hall*　CG：大ホール

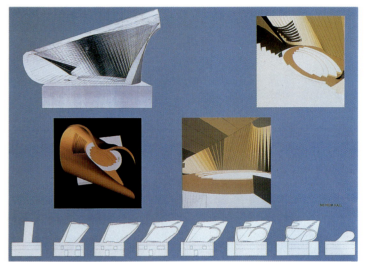

*CG: mobius loop concert hall*　CG：メビウスの帯のホール

*Model: plane of water*

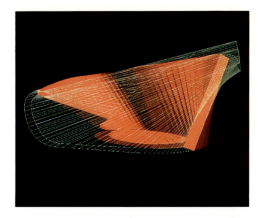

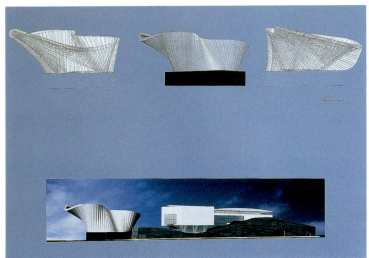

*Geometrical studies*

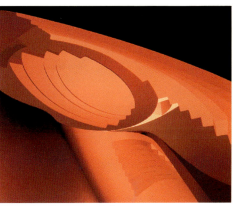

*CG: mobius loop concert hall*

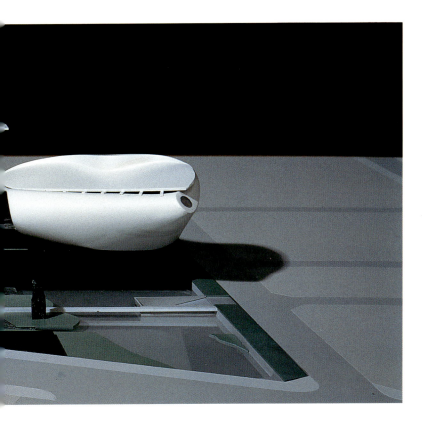

legs or on a base separated from the water and the garden—a dialogue between the elements of nature and the human artefact, which is very interesting in Japan. It's part of the English tradition of the garden but not in the Italian or French tradition. In the Italian and French traditions the garden is part of the architecture; lines, but in infinite extension. I like the dialogue of elements in Zen gardens, the concept of building in rhetorical opposition with nature. This informed the romantic attitude toward nature in the eighteenth century, which came to be important for Ledoux and Schinkel.

**GA:** What about the facilities themselves?

What were you trying to achieve?

**Portzamparc:** I worked principally on two rooms. One is a big concert and congress hall, for which I designed a cube like a city square, with large windows and balconies. I wanted two tiers of balconies so that of an audience of 2000 only 1000 would have to occupy the stalls. I think in a congress hall it is important to be able to sense the presence of the audience. A congress hall is not just the stage but the people who have gathered there, and who may have questions or want to participate in other ways. This hall allows up to 2000 people to feel they are still in an environment that is not too big.

For the other hall I used a Möbius strip inspired by the La Villette ellipse. I wanted to pursue the idea of a place where you have no break in the continuity of the lines and in which you are inside and outside the space at the same time I chose the Möbius strip because it creates a very interesting acoustic phenomenon. Regular vaulted structures give the worst acoustics possible because all the sound is focused in one place. For the ellipse at the Cité de la Musique I had to create niches and organize a rectangular space at the base to avoid this focalizing aspect. With the Möbius strip on the other hand, everything focuses in different directions. You don't

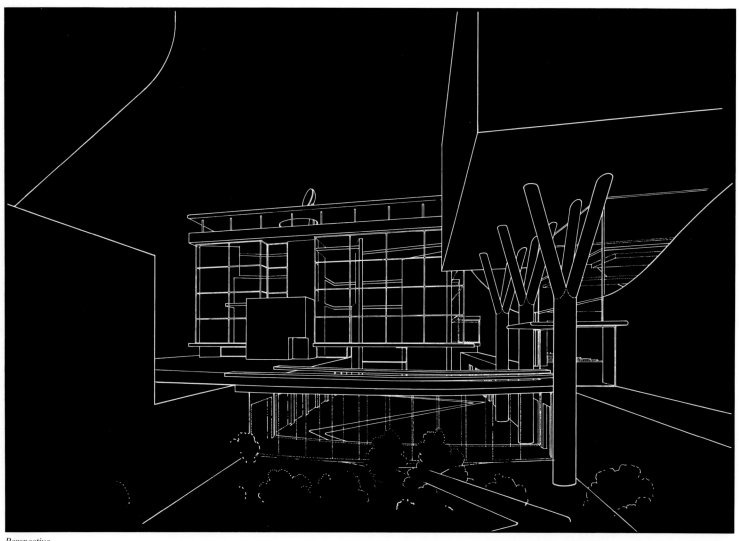

*Perspective*

で，大きな窓とバルコニーの付いた都市広場のようなキューブをデザインしました。2000人の観客のうち1000人が前面の仕切席に座れるように2列のバルコニーを設置したいと思いました。会議場では，聴衆の存在を感じとれることが大切だと思いました。会議場は単なるステージではなく，人々が集まり，質問をしたりあるいは他の方法で参加したいと思うかもしれない場所です。そこでは2000人まで人が入っても，あまりに広すぎる環境のなかにいるとは感じないように配慮してあります。

もう一つのホールでは，ラ・ヴィレットの楕円から発想したメービウスの帯を使いました。線の連続性が断絶しない場所，その内では内部空間と外部空間に同時にいることのできる場所という考えをさらに進めたかったのです。私がメービウスの帯を選んだのは，非常に面白い音響効果をつくりだせるからです。ふつうのヴォールト構造だと音が一点に集中してしまうので最悪の音響となります。音楽都市で楕円をつかったときは，この音の集中を避けるために，ニッチをつくり，基部を矩形にすることが必要でした。一方，メービウスの場合は，すべての音が異なった焦点へ向かいます。単一の焦点では

なくなり，無限の焦点が生まれますが，これは音を操作するのに良い方法なのです。私は，メービウスという私のアイディアは音響効果の点でたぶん非常に良い結果がでるだろうと言う音響専門家と仕事をしました。それで，この理想的なコンサートホールにメービウスの帯を使うという考えを進めることにしました。これは可能なことでした。何故ならプログラムが日本独特のものだったからです。つまり少数の観客のために広い空間を要求していたということで，これはまた日本では観客が高いお金を払うということもあります。ベルリンのシャロウンのコ

have one but an infinite number of focal points, which is a good way to handle sound. I worked with an acoustician who told me that my idea of the Möbius was probably very good acoustically. So I went ahead and tried to make this ideal concert hall using the Möbius strip. This was possible because the program was specifically Japanese, meaning that they wanted a large volume for small audiences, partly because people will pay more in Japan. In Berlin Scharoun's concert hall had to have more than a thousand seats or the philharmonic could not make money. The clients said concerts in Japan are very high level—recordings and so on—so they wanted the best possible acoustics. For good acoustics you need a generous volume, and but a generous volume makes acoustics more difficult. If you build a little hall you have precise acoustics but the sound will never be great, and if you have a big orchestra in a little hall, the sound is often saturated. That's why I fought at La Villette to have high ceilings and a large volume, even though their acoustician wanted low ceilings. In the Möbius band I used reflection in the Möbius band just at the top of the orchestra to create short reflections and diffusion in optimal directions.

**GA:** How did you fit the ceiling in?

**Portzamparc:** I used the ground for the musicians. The audience is on the strip. Part of the strip is shaped to give sounds to the musicians on both sides and the people arriving from below. The roof forms a naturally-lit shed.

**GA:** How about the exterior forms?

**Portzamparc:** I designed the interior without thinking about its exterior ramifications too much. But I knew that it would probably produce something interesting outside. I just worked on the acoustics, and fortunately I liked the exterior outcome. I wanted to oppose a single large shape with these shells and the smaller volume. The three made a very interesting and flexible scheme.

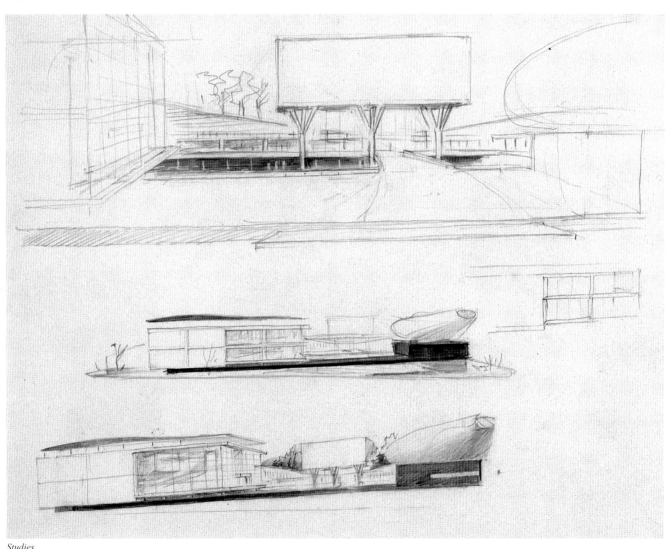

*Studies*

ンサートホールは1000席以上あることが要求されます。さもなければ交響楽団は維持できないのです。クライアントは，日本でのコンサートは非常にレベルが高いので——録音などがありますし——最良の音響を要求してきました。良い音響のためには大きな空間が必要で，また逆に大空間は音響を難しくします。一方，もしホールを小さくすると音響も精確なものとなりますが，音は決して壮大なものにはならないでしょう。小さなホールで大編成のオーケストラを聴いたら，音は飽和状態になってしまいます。ラ・ヴィレットで，音響専門家が低い天井を求めてきたにもかかわらず高い天井と大きな空間にこだわったのはそれが理由です。メービウスの帯のなかでは，オーケストラの最高部のところで短い反響が生まれ，最適な方向に拡散するようにしました。

**GA：**そのなかに天井をどのように設置されたのですか。

**ポルザンパルク：**地上階は音楽家が，聴衆はメービウスの帯のなかに席を占めるようにしました。帯の一部は，演奏者には両側面から，聴衆には下から音が届くような形にしました。屋根は自然光の入る小屋のような形です。

**GA：**外形についてはいかがでしょう。

**ポルザンパルク：**外側があまりに細分化されてしまうということを考えずに内部をデザインしましたが，これはたぶん，外部に面白い何かをつくりだすだろうことも承知していました。音響のことだけを考えていたのですが，幸いにその産物である外形も気に入りました。これらのシェルと小さなヴォリュームに対立する単純な一つの大きな形が面白いと思いました。つまり，この3つの棟は非常に面白く，フレキシブルなスキームをつくりあげていると思います。

# High Court in Grasse
グラスの高等裁判所

Supervisor: Ministère de la Justice   Client: Délégation Générale au Program, Pluriannuel d'Équipement   Program: high court   Structural system: reinforced concrete
Design and construction period: competition winning entry. 1994–   Building area: 25,600 m²   Engineers: SEEE/SDE (structure), OTH  Méditerranée (fluids)   Quantity surveyor: Atec   Contractors: Sogea, Nicoletti

Grasse, France

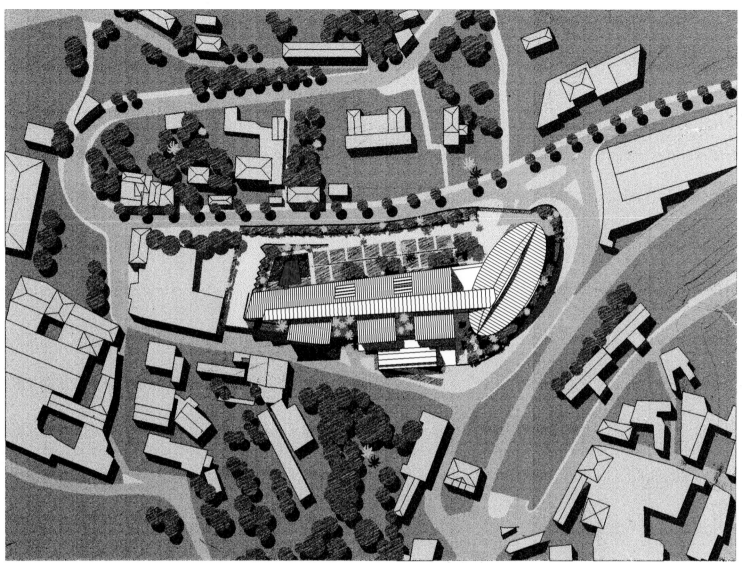

*Site plan*

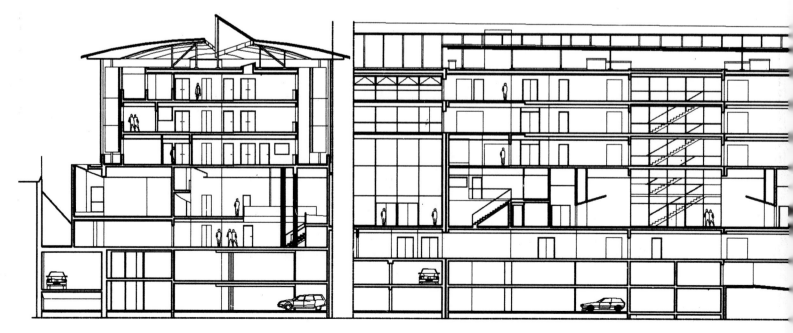

**GA:** This is a series of courtrooms for the city of Grasse. Could you tell me a little bit about it and what your particular concerns were?

**Portzamparc:** The first thing was the site. The city is hilly, with strong differences in level. A long road turns around the site. Behind this road is a high protecting wall.

Two distinct problems are posed here. The site is an elongated one, with a garden, and we had to keep the trees. Secondly, although only part of the site is visible from the city, a court of law has to mark its presence as a major institution there.

Given the elongated site, I divided the program—a civil court for economic litigation, a criminal or assizes court, and a family tribunal—into three distinct parts. The three parts of the court work quite separately, so I didn't have to design a single large building. I then designed a long gallery connecting the three elements with the entrance.

**GA:** Was this in order to create a space where everyone could mingle?

**Portzamparc:** No. Each building has its own lobby, staircase and waiting area. I positioned the civil court close to the road since it doesn't pose any particular security problems. And I placed the smaller, less public family court adjacent to the garden, for greater intimacy.

A court building can be a very tense place to work in, so I tried to palliate the tensions inherent to its activity, although

it had to have a strong institutional presence. A symmetrical form is more common for this type of building, reflecting the idea of justice perhaps. But this wasn't possible here. I decided an ellipse might achieve the required institutional balance. It galvanizes the road and surrounding circulations, focusing attention on the courthouse itself.

Some members of the jury thought the scheme paradoxical—a Baroque image better suited to theater design. I admitted this, but stressed the scheme's contiguous relationship with the long wall, which remains a strong stabilizing factor. And you can see the building from the road, which was essential to the design. It's the only flat road in the city. It had to be possible to read the building's presence from the road.

No other schemes made use of the ellipse, and I think this may have been a key argument in winning over the jury.

**GA:** So the courts are housed in discrete units, but the overall disposition of the volumes and the entry space bind them into a unity.

**Portzamparc:** Yes, I designed a large entrance hall which distributes off to the major and minor elements. There are the appropriate offices above each court. The criminal courts are rectangular. The civil courts are rounder in shape. And the family courts are interestingly lit. The connecting gallery is a long space opening onto a garden—not like a corridor.

**GA:** A glass band wraps around the office

spaces on this facade.

**Portzamparc:** Yes, the offices all receive generous amounts of natural light, using aluminium louvers which can be articulated in three directions and give very good views. I also created a patio here. I wanted natural ventilation, so I incorporated double roofs with air flowing in between.

The city is very proud of the fact that they have this huge height differential between top and bottom, so we tried to exploit this feature. Part of the city overlooks the complex; for instance, the cathedral commands a view over the roofs. I used brick and terracotta for the major elements to match the materials of the urban fabric, and ocher and red as a play on its color scheme.

The moveable cabinets along the garden front modulate natural light according to movement, creating centers of light that can be modified as the users see fit. These could be places where clients meet their lawyers—relatively public places.

**GA:** Is the garden also public?

**Portzamparc:** It belongs to the court but it will have another access too. The garden will be planted with distinct fragrances. There is also a water-course in the manner of gardens in Spain,

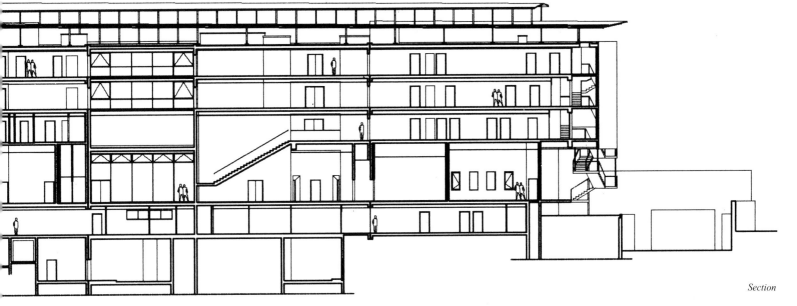

*Section*

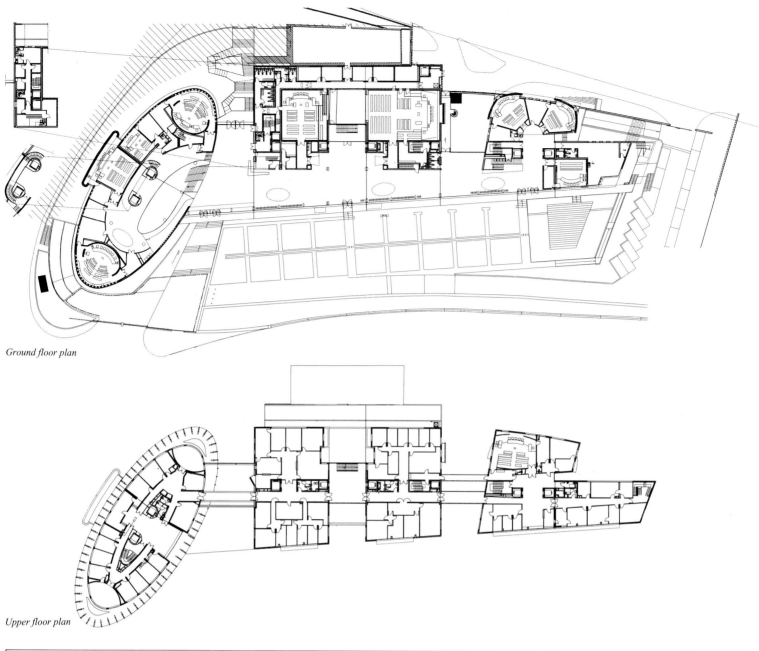

*Ground floor plan*

*Upper floor plan*

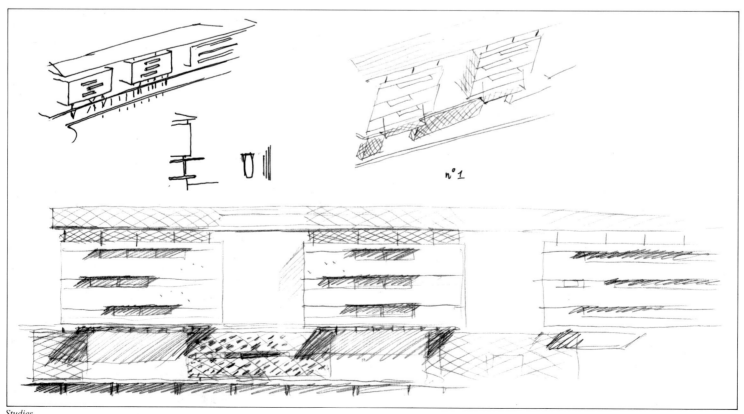

*n° 1*

*Studies*

**GA**：グラス市裁判所の計画であるわけですが，何か特に配慮されたことはありますか。

**ポルザンパルク**：まず敷地が問題でした。グラス市は丘の街で，街全体に強い高低差があります。敷地の周りを長い道が回り込んでいて，この道の片側は高い側壁になっています。

敷地には2つの問題点があります。庭のある細長い敷地で，木立をそのまま残すことが必要です。第2に市内からは敷地のほんの一部しか見えませんが，裁判所ですから市の主要施設であるという存在感が必要となります。

敷地が細長いので，建物を3つに分割しました。経済的な問題を扱う民事裁判所，そして刑事裁判所，家庭裁判所です。これらの法廷での職務は全く異なりますから，一つの大きな建物をつくる必要もなかったわけです。そこでまず，3つの棟を結ぶ，エントランスの付いた長いギャラリーを設計しました。

**GA**：誰もが入り混ざって集まれる場所をつくろうとされたのですか。

**ポルザンパルク**：いいえ，それぞれの建物には専用の階段とウェイティング・スペースの付いたロビーがあります。民事裁判所は，保安上の問題が特にありませんから，通りの近くに配置しました。他より小さく，公共性も少ない家庭裁判所は，心やすい雰囲気にするように，庭に隣接させました。

法廷というのは緊張感の強いものなので，それを和らげるようにしました。機構としての存在感を持たせる必要はありますが，こうしたテンションを高めたくはありませんでした。裁判所は伝統的にシンメトリーな構成になっていることが多いですが，たぶん正義という考えを反映してのことでしょう。しかしここでは，それ

は不可能でした。楕円形が，求められている法廷という場の均衡を表現することができるだろうと決めました。楕円は中心である法廷に注意を集中させながら，道路と周囲のサーキュレーションを活気づけることができます。

コンペ審査員の幾人かはこの計画案は逆説的であり，そのバロック的な様相は劇場などに相応しいと考えました。私はそのことを認めましたが，その建物構成が長い壁と切れ目なくつながり，強い安定性を備えていることを強調しました。道から建物が見えますが，それはこのデザインには本質的なことでした。その道は市内で唯一平坦な道路なのです。道から建物の存在が分かることが必要でした。

楕円を使った案は他にありませんでしたので，これが，審査員の支持を得た主要な根拠になったのかもしれないと思います。

**GA**：各法廷の建物は別になっていますが，ヴォリュームの配置とエントリー・スペースの構成によって全体を統合したわけですね。

**ポルザンパルク**：ええ，大小さまざまな部分へアクセスできるように，この大きなホールをデザインしました。各法廷の上階に事務所があります。刑事法廷は矩形，民事法廷は丸みのある空間，家裁の法廷は採光が楽しいものになっています。全体をまとめているホールは細長い空間で，庭に面しています——廊下のようなものではないわけです。

**GA**：ファサードでは，このガラスの帯がオフィス空間の周囲を包んでいますね。

**ポルザンパルク**：そうです。すべてのオフィスには陽光がたっぷり入り，三方向に角度を調節できるアルミ製のルーヴァーが付いていて，眺めも楽しめます。ここにはパティオもつくりま

した。自然換気にしたいと思いましたので，屋根は二重にして，その間を空気が流れるようにしています。

街の一番低いところから高いところまで，非常な高度差があることを市では自慢にしていましたから，これを生かすことにしました。市の一部はこの建物よりも高い位置にあり，たとえば大聖堂からは裁判所の屋根を見下ろせます。煉瓦やテラコッタを街全体の材料に合わせて主要な部分に使い，黄土色や赤をカラースキームに利用しています。

庭沿いに並ぶ可動のキャビネットは太陽の動きに対応して動かせ，使い手が好きなように日差しを調節できる自然光のセンターのような場をつくりだします。そこは弁護士と依頼人が面会する際にも使えるでしょうし——つまり比較的公共的な場所なのです。

**GA**：庭もパブリックな場所ですか。

**ポルザンパルク**：庭は裁判所に付属していますが，他からも入れるようにするつもりです。良い香りのする植物が植えられ，スペインの庭のように水路もあります。

*Model: hearing room of principal criminal court*　模型：第一刑事法廷の公聴室

*Model: magistrates' court*　模型：下級法廷

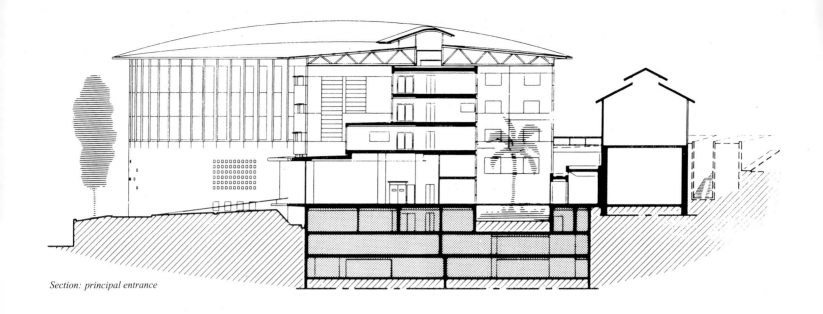

*Section: principal entrance*

*Section: waiting hall*

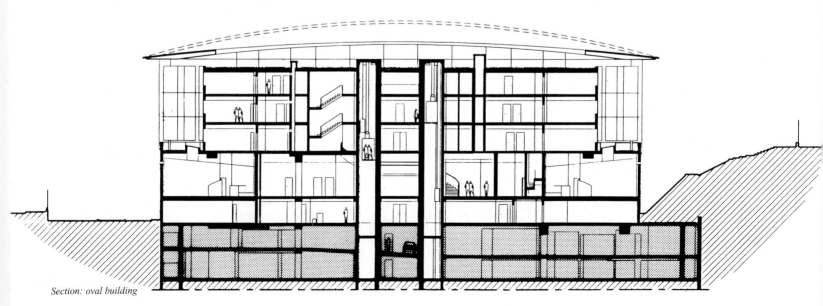

*Section: oval building*

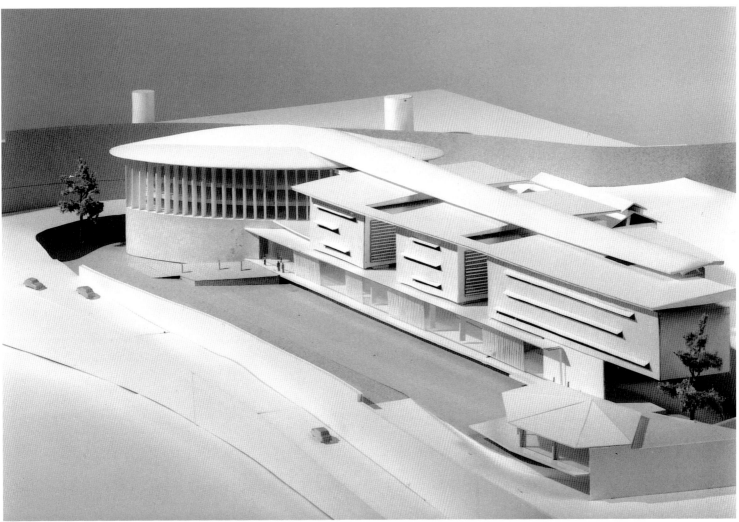

*Model*

*Model*

# New Cultural Center
レンヌ文化センター

Client: City of Rennes   Program: new cultural center for the city of Rennes regrouping a library, the Brittany museum, and a cultural center for science, industry and technology Design year: competition winning entry. 1993 (studies in progress)   Structural system: reinforced concrete   Building area: 34,600 m²   Engineers: Sodetec

Rennes, France

*Study*

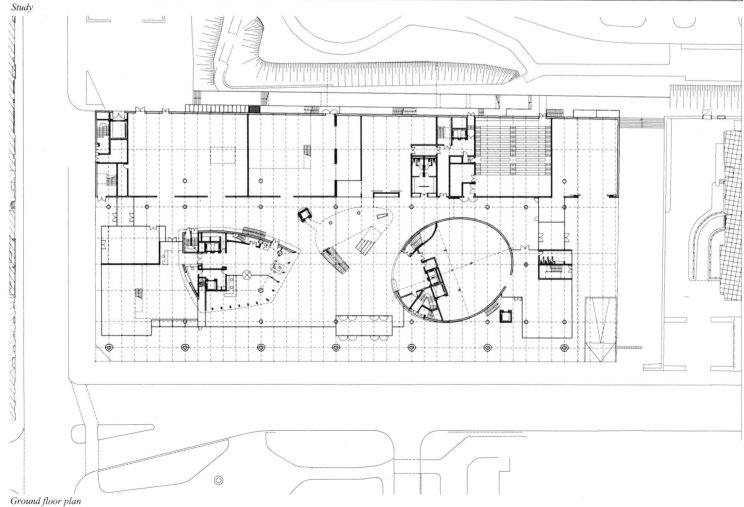

*Ground floor plan*

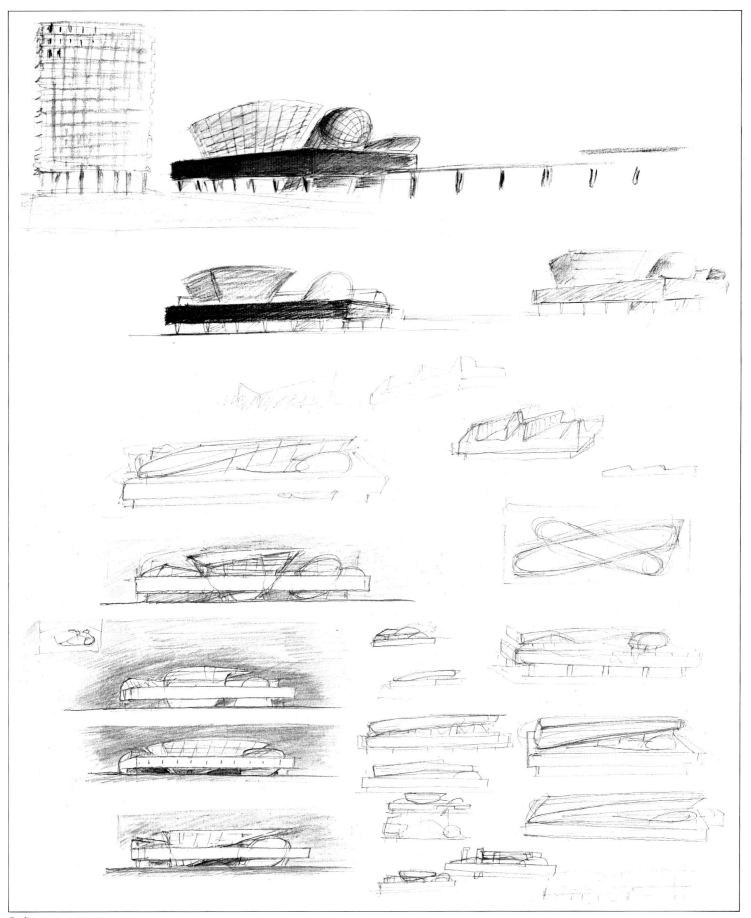

*Studies*

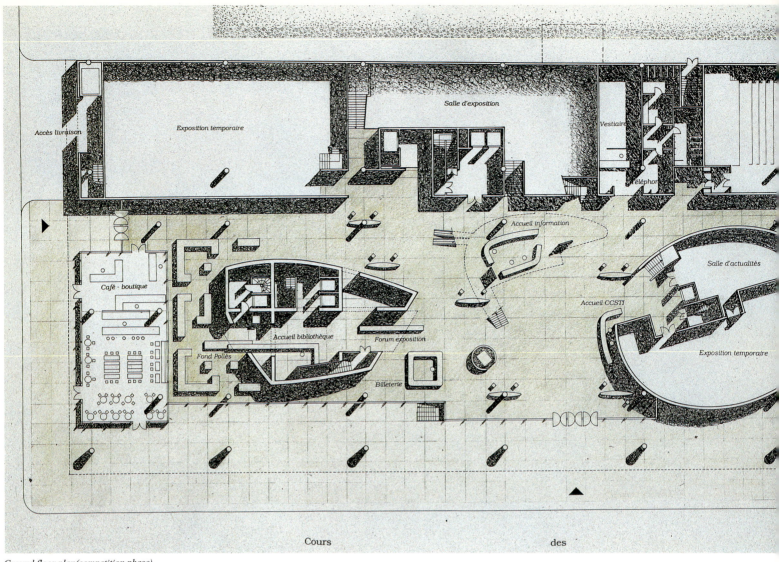

Exposition temporaire

Salle d'exposition

Accès livraison

Vestiaire

Téléphon

Accueil information

Café - boutique

Salle d'actualités

Accueil CCSTI

Fond Pollès

Accueil bibliothèque

Forum exposition

Exposition temporaire

Billeterie

Cours                                                    des

*Ground floor plan(competition phase)*

**Portzamparc:** Here, large parts of the city center were "renovated" in the sixties and seventies and became rather depressing, like the cities of Eastern Europe. The center is quite different from the feeling of the little Breton town with its interesting historical neighborhoods on the other side of the river. The competition was for a building comprising three institutions; a new public library, the Museum of Brittany, and a Cultural Center for Science and Technology. These three institutions already exist in the city. I worked on two themes; one was that the building should be able to transform the space. Right now the site is a huge parking area which was a military camp before, several uninteresting buildings. I tried to imagine how this huge empty lot could be transformed into something remarkable. The location itself is very good, with a station nearby and the river just 300 meters away. The neighborhood is not as pleasant as it used to be, but it still has a lot of residents. I used to live in this town. I finished my studies near

here. So I know its past very well. I worked a long time on this project before finding the solution just before the competition deadline. During the first three months I kept rearranging things without really grasping a strong idea. I didn't want to put all the program in one big suitcase because I thought that each of the institutions would lose individual identity and they might end up competing with each other.

**GA:** Are you talking about images internally or externally?

**Portzamparc:** Both. The idea is that this public will be activated by synergetic relationships. People visiting the library will discover the museum and then might go on to the museum. The public and the various institutions will benefit from being together. There will be a new public domain and more people will be attracted to this part of the city. But I was aware that for this to succeed, the three parts would each have to be recognizable. I thought that if they each had their own homes they would

be happy to be close together. It's very similar to my thinking about the separate parts of Cité de la Musique. There are three different programs on which I worked separately and for which I created different shapes. I tried to create a geography whereby they can recognize the other. They are not just anonymous rooms in a large homogeneous container. Hence, the feeling and power of the forms are important even if they do not look like traditional volumes. Each should have a sense of identity. I had these concepts in mind but I had to work on the forms for a long time. I wanted separate identities but I wanted the three to be, at the same time, one. Three in one, one in three. In the end I decided the museum would be a flat horizontal block with all the rooms beside each other. Everyone wanted to have space on the ground floor since they are all public institutions, but I said the library only required a lobby—a discreet footprint—with the main space on the upper floors. The form for the science museum came

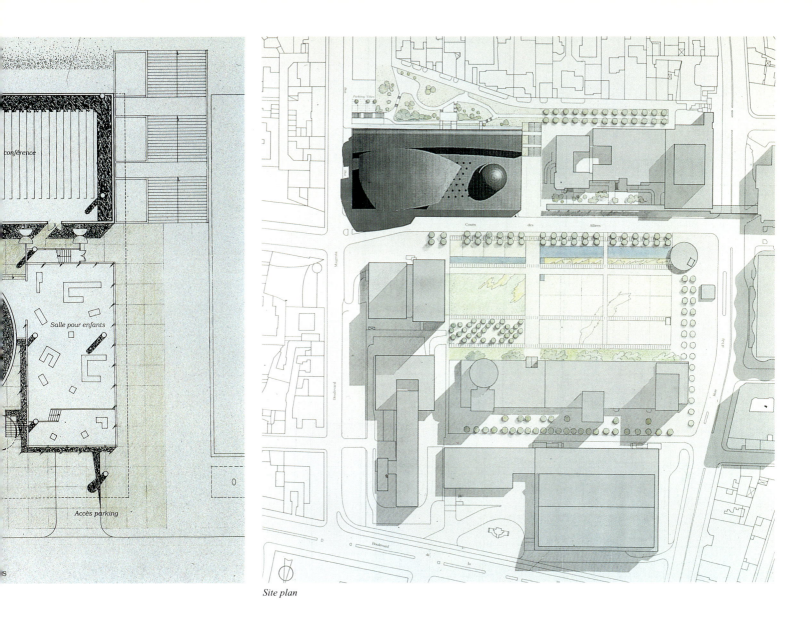

*Site plan*

because they needed an exhibition hall on the ground floor, some on the upper floors, and a planetarium at the top. The outside is also important. There is a bridge at the level of the museum from which you can enter the library or the scientific museum. The light entering through little holes make it a living space where people can understand the forms. There is a café, a mezzanine, and a library annex where they will read newspapers from all around the world every day. It could be an interesting place for young students or people who are working on something specific. The museum includes exhibition halls, a lecture hall, a cafeteria, and a library for children. There is also a play area for children, equipped with scientific machines. This is something which is popular in France: machines for children. The children can experiment with fish, computers and scientific phenomena. Then of course there are the administrative offices. I was also careful to position the windows so that the museum had views of the city.

**GA:** What do you have in mind for the exterior materials? And what are your strategies for the building's impact on the surroundings?

**Portzamparc:** The materials will be colored in light granite, gray-green metal, and maybe another gray. I'm still working on this. Maybe it could be all light gray. I might decide that the forms are strong enough on there own and that it's not necessary to use color. Around the facilities I proposed placing water and trees. Parking is underground. The long flat museum will be a response to the tower. I wanted something also a rectangle within rectangles, a sculptural shape which would be a good counterpoint in this interplay of forms. The horizontals will enhance the difficult verticality of the tower, which is a little top-heavy. My volume is similar, but laid out flat. The lines help to understand the horizontal spaces. It's interesting for me that a building in a space can modify the presence of other buildings around it. This is my goal with this building.

**GA:** The scale of the building, and how you composed the spaces according to the city plan, seem to me a very Corbusian way to achieve the program. They remind me of the congress hall at Chandigarh, especially in its ground floor plan.

**Portzamparc:** Perhaps the museum could be a Villa Savoye type of situation, with a flat pure band and a free plan on the ground floor with pilotis. You are right. I was not conscious of this but it is obviously part of the French architectural heritage, which certainly influences my work. I have no knowledge of Corbusian work with intersecting elements but it's clear he must have influenced my work. In this case, I was interested in levitating this part off the ground. For me, this was a correct response to the top-heavy tower on the adjacent site. The result is different, but it is true that one of the schemes—with its free plan and the pilotis—could be interpreted as Corbusian.

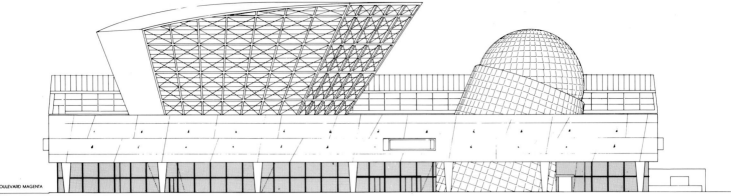

*Elevation*

ポルザンパルク：ここでは都市の中心部にある広い地区が60年代，70年代に"一新"されてきたのですが，東ヨーロッパのように，活気を失ってしまっていました。川の対岸に楽しい歴史地区のあるブルターニュの小さな都市とはその雰囲気がまったく違っています。コンペでは，3つの施設からなる建物を要求していました。新しい公共図書館，ブルターニュ美術館，科学技術センターです。これらの3つの施設は既にこの街にあるものです。私は2つのテーマをもって設計しました。一つは，建物がこの空間を変貌させることができるものとすること。現在，元は軍のキャンプだったこの地区は広大な駐車場になっていて，いくつかのつまらない建物があります。この広大な空っぽの場所が，どうしたら素晴らしいものとなるだろうかを想像するようにしました。ロケーションそのものはなかなか良いのです。駅も近いですし，川は300m先を流れています。周囲はかつてほど気持ちよいものではありませんが，まだたくさんの住宅が建っています。私はこの街に住んでいたことがあり，この近くの学校を卒業しましたから，昔の姿はよく知っています。この設計案を思いつくまでに，コンペ締切りの直前まで長い時間がかかりました。最初の3ヶ月は，有力なアイディアをつかめないままに，いろいろと再構成を繰り返していました。すべてのプログラムを一つの大きなスーツケースのなかにまとめてしまいたくありませんでした。それぞれの施設は独自性を失いお互いが競い合うのを止めてしま

うと思ったからです。

GA：それは内部についてでしょうか，それとも外部についてですか。

ポルザンパルク：両方です。このパブリック・スペースは共働的関係によって活気づくというのがアイディアです。図書館に来た人は美術館があるのに気づき，ここも見て行く気になるかもしれません。公共施設はまとまっていることによってお互いに利益を得るでしょう。ここは新しい公共領域となり，前より人々が引きつけられてくるでしょう。一方，これを成功させるためには，3つの部分はそれぞれ見分けられるようにすべきだということにも気づいていました。各自がそれぞれの本拠をもつことで，間近にいても幸せな気分でいられるのだと思います。これは音楽都市の各部を離しておくという考えと同様のものです。別々に作業し，異なった形態をもたせた3つのプログラムがあります。お互いを認識できる地形をつくるようにしました。均質で大きなコンテナのなかの単なる無名の空間ではないのです。ですから，形態の雰囲気と力が，たとえ伝統的なヴォリュームのように見えないにせよ重要なのです。それぞれが独自性をもたねばなりません。こうしたコンセプトを考えていましたが，形態を決めるには時間がかかりました。それぞれが個性的であると同時に3つは一つである必要があります。一つで3つ，3つで一つということです。結局，美術館は，すべての部屋が互いに隣接する，平坦で水平なものにすることにしました。3つの

すべてが公共施設でしたから，それぞれ1階にある程度のスペースをほしがりましたが，図書館が1階に必要とするのはロビーだけだと説得して，1階は少しの床面積として上階を広くとることにしました。1階と2階に展示空間，そして屋上にはプラネタリウムが必要ということから科学館の形が生まれました。

外観も大切でした。美術館レベルにブリッジがあり，そこから図書館や科学館に入れます。小さな穴から差し込む光がこの空間を生き生きさせ，人々がその形を理解できるようなものにしています。カフェ，中2階，図書館分室があり，そこでは毎日世界中の新聞を見ることができます。若い学生や専門領域をもつ市民には魅力のある場所になるはずです。ミュージアムにはいくつかの展示ホール，講義室，カフェテリア，子供のための図書室があります。科学的な装置が設置された子供たちが遊べる場所もあります。子供たちのための機械というのは，フランスではポピュラーです。子供たちは，魚や，コンピュータや，その他の科学現象を実地に試すことができるのです。そしてもちろん，管理事務室があります。窓の位置を注意深く設定したので，ミュージアムからも市街が見晴らせます。

GA：外壁の材料にはどんなものを考えているのですか。また，周囲に対する建物のもつインパクトについてはどのようなストラテジーをお持ちですか。

ポルザンパルク：明るい色の花崗岩，灰緑色の金属を使うことになるでしょう，そしてたぶん

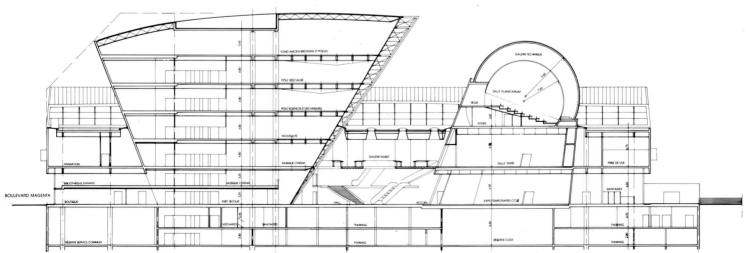

*Longitudinal section*

別種の灰色も。これはまだ検討中です。すべてが明るい灰色になるかもしれません。形態が充分に強いので，色彩を使う必要はないかもしれません。施設の周囲には水や木立を配置することを提案しています。駐車場は地下になります。長く平坦なミュージアムは隣接するタワーへの応答であり，長方形のなかのもう一つの長方形という形態の相互作用のなかで，恰好の対旋律になるような彫刻的な形態がほしかったのです。水平性は，頭の方が少し重すぎるタワーの垂直性の危うさを強調するかもしれません。私の設計したヴォリュームにもそれと似た形がありますが，平坦に広がっています。これらの線は水平の空間を理解する助けとなると思います。一つの空間内にある一つの建物が，それを囲む他の建物の存在を調停することができるということは面白いものです。これが，この建物に対する私の目標です。

**GA**：建物の大きさと，都市プランに従って空間を構成していくというやり方は，プログラムを解くにあたって，非常にコルビュジエ的な方法のように思います。チャンディガールの議事堂，特にその1階のプランを連想させます。

**ポルザンパルク**：たぶん，美術館はサヴォワ邸タイプの状況にあるかもしれません。その内に人の住まう，平坦で純粋な帯，そして1階のピロティと自由平面。君の言う通りです。意識していませんでしたが，それは明らかにフランス人建築家の遺産の一つであり，確かに，これらのコンセプトのいくつかが，私の作品のなかに入ってきています。交差するエレメントをもったコルビュジエ風の作品については知りませんが，彼が私の建物に影響を与えているに違いないことは確かです。このプロジェクトでは，この部分を地上から離して空中に浮かび上がらせることに関心がありました。私にはこれが，隣の敷地にある頭の重いタワーへの正しい応答だったのです。生まれた結果は違っていますが，フリープランとピロティをもった計画案の一つが，コルビュジエ派としての翻訳であることは事実です。

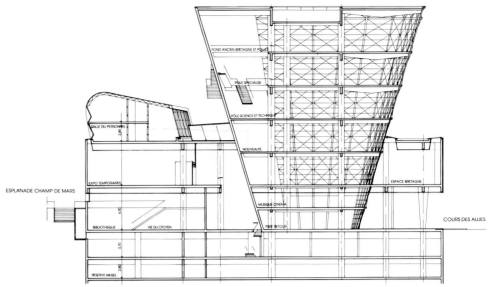

*Section: inverted pyramid*

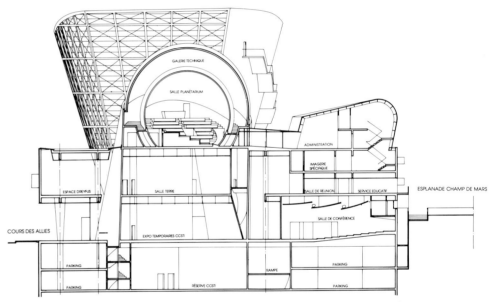

*Section: planetarium*

*Model*

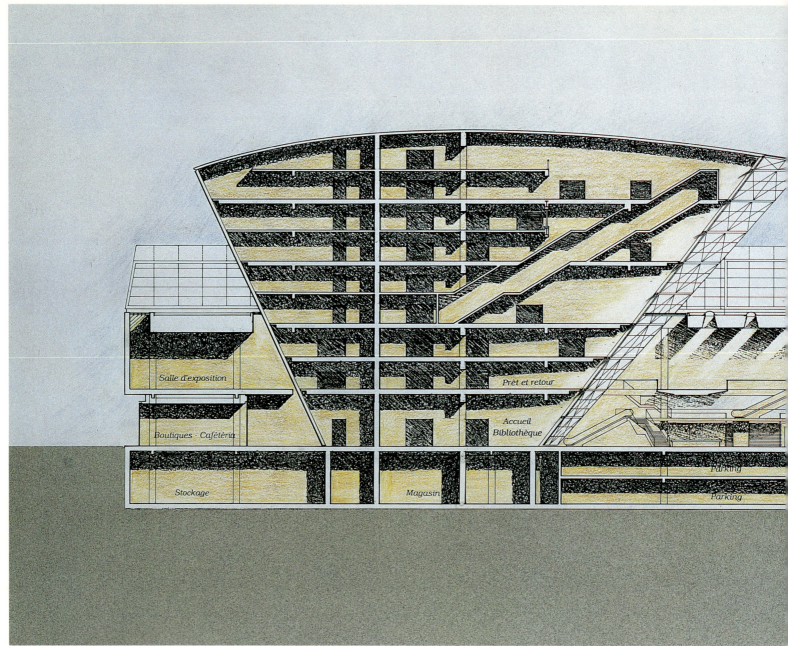

Salle d'exposition

Prêt et retour

Boutiques · Cafétéria

Accueil
Bibliothèque

Stockage

Magasin

Parking

Parking

*Section: museum of Brittany, public library, & culture center for science and technology*

*Perspective: general entrance*

Salle hémisphérique

Foyer

Salle du patrimoine

Exposition

Exposition

Salle pour enfants

Parking

Parking

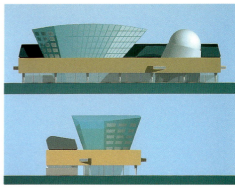

*Elevations*

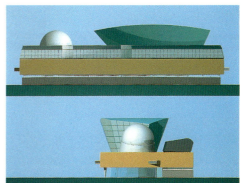

*Elevations*

139

# Bandai Cultural Complex
## バンダイ文化センター

Client: Bandai Co., Ltd.   Program: cultural center (300-seat concert hall), restaurant, offices, housing   Design year: competition winning entry. 1994 (studies in progress)
Structural system: reinforced concrete   Area: 7,000 m²

Tokyo, Japan

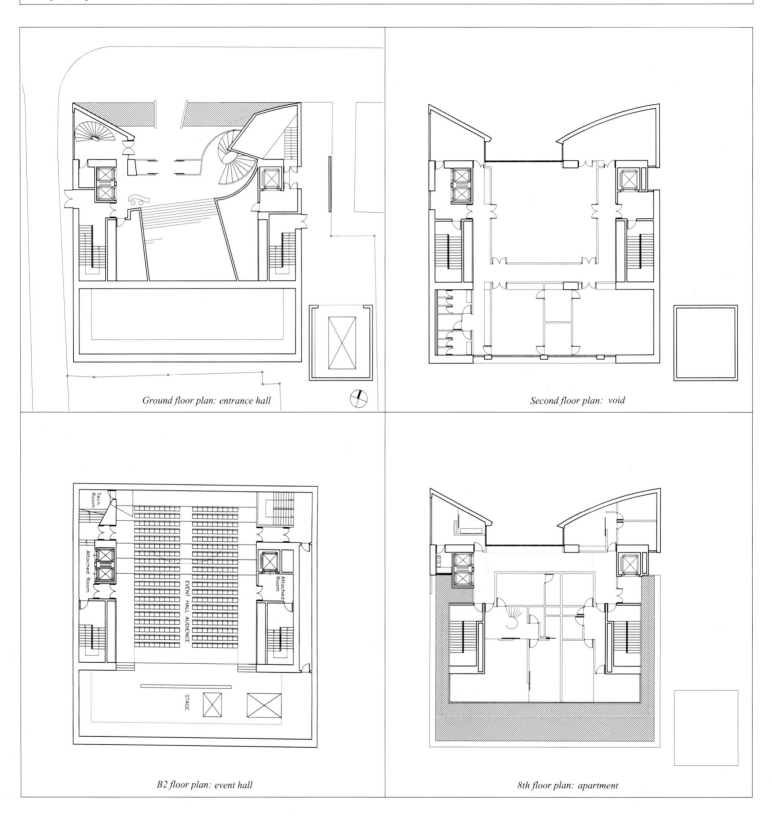

Ground floor plan: entrance hall

Second floor plan:  void

B2 floor plan: event hall

8th floor plan: apartment

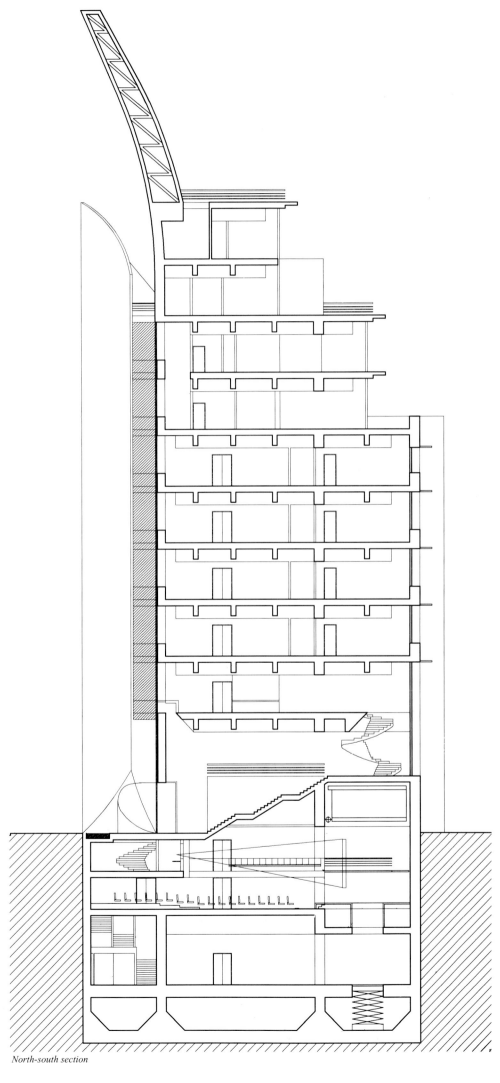

*North-south section*

**GA:** Tell me why you and Jean Nouvel were chosen for this competition.

**Portzamparc:** I don't know really. I think the advisor of the company was interested in using a French architect. We went together to see the client and to look at the site, and three months later we went back to present the project together. It was very friendly. Jean's project was black and mine was white. His was rectangular and mine was wavy. Everything was diametrically opposed. Maybe they thought it would be interesting to see two different approaches to the same problem.

**GA:** Tell me about the program.

**Portzamparc:** It's basically a cultural center but it also has apartments on the top. You enter a large foyer, and the first large event hall is underground. There is a restaurant/bar above the entrance hall, and a second event hall above that. Then there is a series of multi-purpose rooms that could be used for offices or events like fashion shows, movies, special shows, advertising, merchandising, cultural events, etc. These are on the fourth, fifth, sixth and seventh floors. Above this I placed a restaurant with a good view, and finally, above this is a village of apartment units.

**GA:** I see that the volumes of the apartments are stepped back as you go up. The apartments are encased in a glass box. Is

**GA**：どういういきさつであなたとジャン・ヌヴェルがこのコンペに選ばれたのですか。

**ポルザンパルク**：実のところよく分からないのです。この会社に助言されている方がフランス人の建築家を使いたいと思われたのではないでしょうか。二人でクライアントに会いに行き，敷地を見て，三ヶ月後にまた二人で計画案を提示しに行きました。二人仲良くね。ジャンの案は黒，私の案は白。彼のは矩形，私のは曲線。すべてが逆でした。彼らは同じ問題に対する2つの異なった答えを見るのは面白いと考えたのかもしれません。

**GA**：プログラムはどういうものですか。

**ポルザンパルク**：基本的には文化センターですが，最上階はアパートです。まず壮大なエントリーホールに入ると，最初のイヴェント用大ホールが地下にあります。エントランスホールの上階にレストラン／バーがあり，2番目のイヴェント・ホールがさらにその上にあります。4，5，6，7階には，オフィスやファッションショー，映画，宣伝，商業目的あるいは文化的なイヴェントに利用できる，多目的ホールが連なっています。8階はすばらしい展望を楽しめるレストラン，そして最後に，アパート・ユニットの並ぶ"村"がくるわけです。

**GA**：アパートのユニットは上に向かってステップバックしていき，ガラス箱に封じ込められ

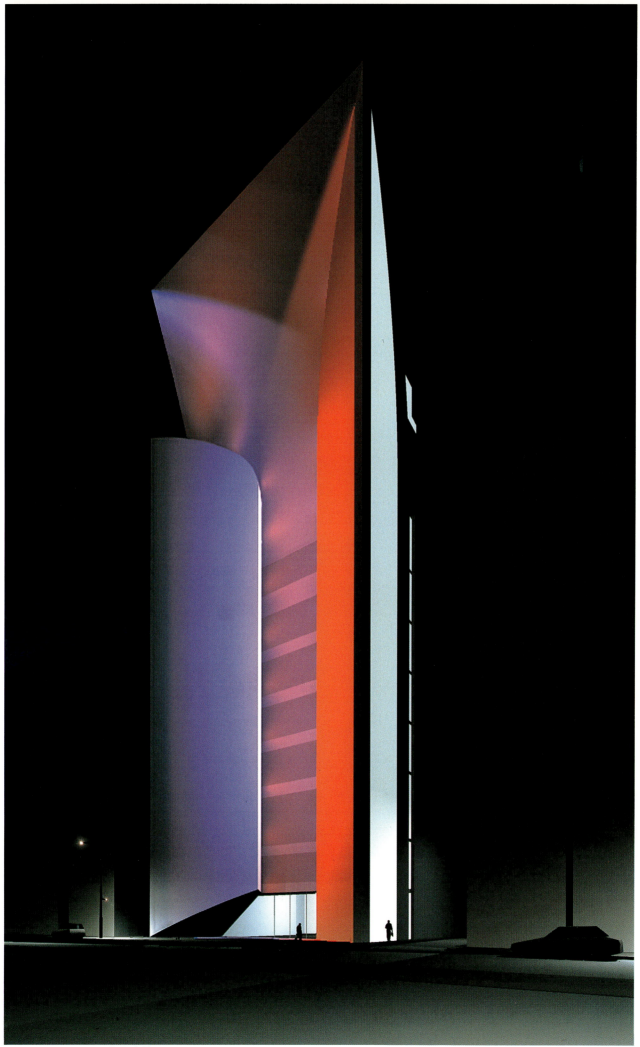

*CG: view from northwest*　北西より見る

there a particular reason for this?

**Portzamparc:** They descend in scale because we were obliged to follow zoning restrictions. It ends up like a village of apartments above a tower which serves as its base. The apartments are just floors surrounded by glass and panels. They're not completely open, but that's the concept.

**GA:** What was your strategy for the building's presence along the boulevard?

**Portzamparc:** I thought it was important to express the fact that this is a cultural center, a multi-purpose building along Aoyama Boulevard. It shouldn't look like your normal office building. I wanted something eventful. The sculptural event in the atrium acts like a magnet, a bit like Maki's Spiral Building, but in another way.

**GA:** The Spiral Building is also very sculptural. Maki's design is an attempt to represent the movement of the people toward the street, but you never show the inside to the outside.

**Portzamparc:** That's true. I wanted something that would catch the eye through the building's scale and its attitude to the street and the Tokyo cityscape.

**GA:** Many foreign architects have been fascinated by the lights and neon signs on the high rises of Tokyo.

**Portzamparc:** Yes, I also admire the fantastic imagery, the use of light and color for advertising. I thought this could be an interesting theme—Tokyo as a city of light and color. But here I decided not use light and color as advertisement, but electric color as pure media—advertising media transformed into fine art. I wanted to pursue the theme of the niches of my concert hall at La Villette and the first prototype I made for an exhibition eight years ago. The interplay of colors—how the colors gradually change—was very interesting and I wanted to introduce this into this project. For example, every evening for a half and hour or so, an artist could orga-

nize an improvised light show, or else it could be computerized. Not just color but color in motion. I think it could be quite interesting on an urban scale. People might come here just to watch the event for its ten-minute or half-hour duration. It could potentially become a popular thing, like fireworks. We are using animated CAD to show how this might work

**GA:** It seems the building will be very different in the day time. Did you focus mostly on what the building would be like at night?

**Portzamparc:** Perhaps I focused more on the evening—a cultural center whose events would take place mostly in the evening. But I also think the sculptural form will be an interesting landmark in the daytime.

**GA:** You bent the facade at a right angle to the avenue. Did you think about the direction from the avenue, where people may come by car?

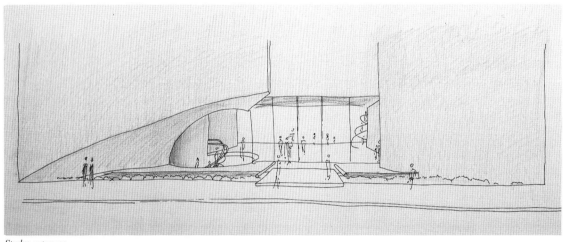

*Study: entrance*

ていますね。何か特別な理由があるのですか。

**ポルザンパルク:** 上へ行くほど小さくなっているのはゾーニング法のためであり，結局タワーを基壇として重なるアパート・ユニットの集落のようになりました。アパートはガラスやパネルで囲んだだけのもので，完全に開放的であるわけではありませんが，それがここでのコンセプトでした。

**GA:** 大通りに面した建築表現に対するストラテジーについてはいかがでしょう。

**ポルザンパルク:** 青山通りに面する文化センターであり，多目的ビルであるということを表現することが重要でした。平凡なオフィスビルのような外観にすべきではありません。何かさまざまなことが発生する場所にしたいと思いました。アトリウムのなかの彫刻的イヴェントは，磁石のような作用をし，槇さんのスパイラルビルと多少似ていますが，別な方法です。

**GA:** スパイラルビルもとても彫刻的です。槇さんのデザインは人々の動きを道路に向かって表現しようとしていますが，あなたの建物では内部を外部に見せていませんね。

**ポルザンパルク:** その通りです。私のは建物のスケールと，街路や東京の都市景観への対し方によって人々の注目を惹こうというものです。

**GA:** 来日した多くの建築家が，東京の高層建築群に瞬く照明やネオンサインの効果に興味をもちますね。

**ポルザンパルク:** 広告に使われている照明や色彩のつくりだす幻想的なイメージは素晴らしいですね。光と色彩都市としての東京というテーマは面白いものになると思います。しかしここでは，照明や色を広告ではなく，その電子カラーを純粋なメディアとして使うことにしました——広告メディアを美術に変貌させるのです。ラ・ヴィレットのコンサートホールで試みたニッチ，8年前に展覧会用に制作したその最初のプロトタイプのためのテーマをさらに追求してみたかったのです。色彩の相互作用，ゆっくりと色が変化していく様相がとても面白かったので，このプロジェクトでも使いたいと思いました。たとえば演奏家やアーティストが毎晩30分か1時間ぐらい，即興によるライトショーを行うとか，あるいはコンピュータ制御でやっても

よいのです。単に色というのではなく，動いていく色です。都市のスケールに対しとても面白いものになると思います。誰かを立ち止まらせ10分くらい見つめさせてしまうような何か。この10分あるいは30分間のショーを見るために足を運ぶ人も出てくるかもしれません。花火のようなポピュラーなものになる可能性もあります。これがどのように演じられるか見るために，CADのアニメーションを使っています。

**GA:** 日中には建物は大きく違ってきそうですね。夜に建物がどのように見えるかを重視したのですか。

**ポルザンパルク:** そうですね。どちらかというと夜の方に注目したかもしれません。文化センターでは，主に夜にイヴェントが行われますから。これはとても重要なことでした。しかし，日中の彫刻的な形もまたランドマークとして目を引くものになると思います。

**GA:** ファサードを大通りに対し直角に曲げていますね。人々が車で来るかもしれない大通りからの方向について配慮したのですか。

**ポルザンパルク:** 大きく掘り抜いた部分があ

**Portzamparc:** I worked on several models, with the idea that the building would have a large hollowed-out portion, with colored lights at night, but also that it would catch the light well during the day. The clients said that there was the possibility of appropriating more land behind the building in the future, and so I wanted the base to be transparent to provide visual extension toward the back. The windows also allow the multi-purpose rooms to open up. It was important to me that this sculptural arrangement would not be hidden from the boulevard—that you could understand the volume of the multiple halls and offices and the housing village. I was careful to position the forms so that they could be seen from the streets. In this way, you are afforded a better view of the light display. The facade is not symmetrical, there's a flat angle and a rounded part, and the light radiates from within the niches.

**GA:** I heard that the facade is patterned on a Gingko tree leaf, the emblem of Tokyo.

**Portzamparc:** It's an amusing story. I asked a Japanese architect I know in Paris to come to my office so that I could ask him about building regulations in Tokyo. He saw the drawings and said, this is the leaf of Tokyo, this is very good. I said fine. It was not intentional but if the client is happy I welcome the idea.

り，夜にはさまざまな色の光があたる，という アイディアによる模型をいくつかつくってみま したが，それはまた，昼間の光も十分に捕らえ るでしょう。クライアントは将来増築可能なだ けの土地が裏手にあると言っていましたので， 基部を透明性の高いものにして後ろの方に視界 が広がるようにしたかったのです。また，多目 的室を開放的なものにするために窓をとりまし た。建物の彫刻的構成が通りから隠れてしまわ ないこと，多目的ホールやオフィス，そして "集落"のようなアパート・ユニットのヴォリュ ームが判読できることが大切でした。形態の配 置を非常に注意して決めましたので，通りから よく見えることになるでしょう。これによって， 光の演出が良く見えることになります。建物は 左右対称ではなく，平坦な角度，円みのある部 分があり，ニッチから光が放射されます。

**GA：**このファサードは東京都のシンボルであ る銀杏の葉の形をしていると聞きましたが。

**ポルザンパルク：**おかしな話なのです。東京の 建築法規について聞こうと，パリにいる日本人 建築家にオフィスに来てくれるように頼みまし た。彼は私の図面を見て，これは素敵だ。東京 の銀杏の葉ですよと言うのです。私は，それは 良かったと言いました。意図したわけではあり ませんが，クライアントが歓迎なら，このアイ ディアも良しということです。

*North elevation*

*Studies: entrance*

*West elevation*

*South elevation*

*Color studies for illumination at night*
カラー・イルミネーションのスタディ

# School of Architecture in Marne-la-Vallée
## マルヌ・ラ・ヴァレの建築学校

Client: Ministère de l'Équipement des Transport et du Tourisme　Program: competition for the new school of architecture in Marne la Vallée for 500 students in the first phase, and 1,200 students in the second phase　Design period: 1994　Area: 14,480 m²　Program design: Interconsultculture　Quantity surveyor: Atec

Marne-la-Vallée, France

**Portzamparc:** This school is located in Marne-la-Vallée. My question was what would the appropriate strategy be for a school in this town which is not a traditional town, but a new town. The urban character of the surroundings is not particularly lively. The site is also located a long way from the station—a problem for the students. Hence, it was important to create a good environment. We tried to exploit the qualities of the site, which is full of beautiful trees. At the same time, I recognized that the school had to be more or less protected and isolated. My approach stemmed partly from my work on the School of Beaux-Arts, which I completed some time ago, and which was also on a very cramped site. In this project I had separated one project which contains an amphitheater, a heavy materials workshop and a library, and another site on top of this first building, comprising a workshop which is open to the light and organized an enfilade outside, like a little village of workshops.

**GA:** So you used similar principles of organization?

**Portzamparc:** This time I organized the project horizontally into three levels, lower, common connecting level, and an upper level with workshops. Then I divided it lengthwise into three islands with open spaces between them. One of these is a water pond enclosed by a cloister, and the other is part of an existing wooded area through which glass corridors linking Isles 2 & 3 will pass. In the summer, when the leaves are thick, you won't be able to see the other building across the space and it will be like passing through a cloud.

**GA:** I see you have given each of the major volumes and open spaces their own character.

**Portzamparc:** We wanted the school to be a major presence in the neighborhood. It had to be an important base for students and the community because it is so far removed from the center of the city. The program called for spaces for about 1500 pupils but I considered that the total community could grow to around 4000. My first proposal was very dense and not open anywhere. By adding two voids the interior was opened to the light and more im-

**ポルザンパルク：**この建築学校はマルヌ・ラ・ヴァレにあります。伝統のある古い街ではなく、ニュータウンに建設する学校にはどのようなストラテジーが適切か、というのが私の課題でした。周囲の都市環境はそれほど活気に満ちたものではありませんし、敷地も駅から遠く、学生には歓迎されない条件です。そこで、良い環境をつくることがとても大切なことになり、美しい木立に囲まれているという利点を生かすことにしました。同時に、学校とは多かれ少なかれ、保護され孤立した空間でなければならないことも承知していました。私のアプローチは、一部には私がしばらく前に、同じように狭い敷地にボザールの学校を設計したときに考えたことか らきていました。そのときは、階段教室、重材料のワークショップと図書館から成る一つのプロジェクトを他のものから分けて構成し、この建物の上をもう一つの敷地と考え、ここに外光に向けて開放されたワークショップを、縦に通るサーキュレーションをその外側に回して、小さな集落のように配置しました。

**GA：**同じような構成原則を使ったわけですね。

**ポルザンパルク：**このプロジェクトでは、水平に３つのレヴェルに分けました。下階、共通する連絡階、ワークショップのある上階に分かれています。次に敷地の長手方向に３つのアイランド、つまり３つの棟に分け、その間はオープンスペースとなります。そのうちひとつは回廊 に囲まれた池、もうひとつには既存の木立を残し、そのなかをアイランド２と３を連絡するガラスで包まれた廊下が渡っています。夏に木々が厚く茂ると建物は見えなくなり、まるで雲のなかを通っていくような感じになるでしょう。

**GA：**それぞれの建物とオープンスペースに異なった性格を与えたわけですね。

**ポルザンパルク：**大学が地域の主要な存在になって欲しいと思いました。市の中心からあまりに遠いので、近隣周辺や学生たちの大切な拠点になる必要があったのです。プログラムでは生徒数約1500人を想定していましたが、私はこのコミュニティは合わせて4000人にまで膨らむ可能性があると考えました。最初の提案は高密度

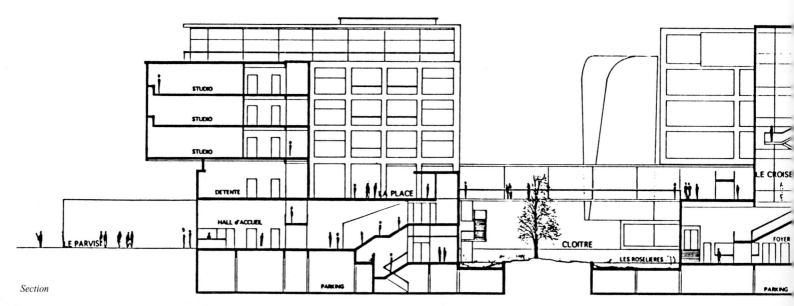

*Section*

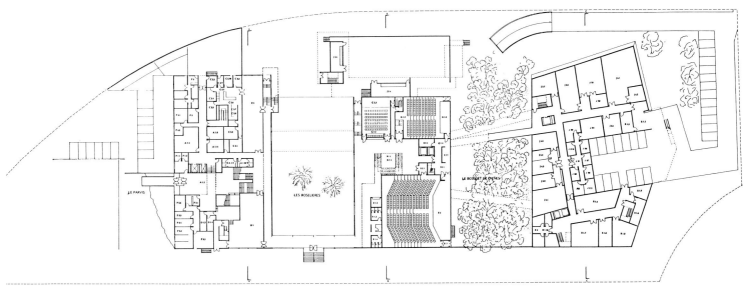

*Ground floor plan*

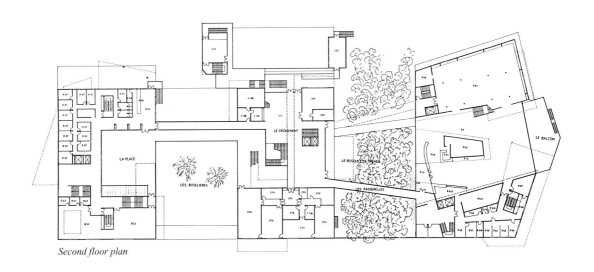

*Second floor plan*

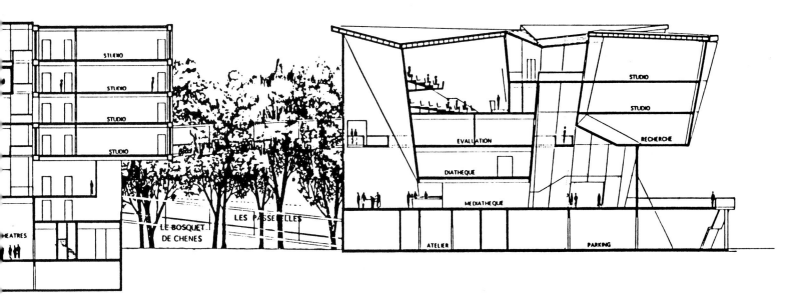

*Model: overall view*

*View from east*

*Island 3(library): west elevation*

*Island 3(library)*

*Island 1*

*Island 3(library): south elevation*

portantly made it possible to differentiate the three new volumes spatially and formally. This led to the introduction of my next idea which was to deal with variation. Initially, I was asked to make the school as neutral as possible: gray or white, I believe. But for me this was inappropriate for a building that was to hold so many people. I thought the importance of the building makes the aspect of its presence critical. I knew highly specific spaces would leave a strong impression on the students, especially first-year students of architecture. I thought that the spaces themselves could be a good introduction to the field. They could sense how the organization of forms and space could effect perception. It is something they would be testing slowly during their studies. But I also felt that, with this potential in mind, the vision of one architect was perhaps too authoritarian. Today we don't have just one architecture, one possibility or one style, we have many. So I had the idea of having a different architect for each island. I wanted to ask two of my colleagues to design the other ones, but this proved complicated for the competition. Money and deadlines made it hard to manage, so I decided to do it myself. It would be like an exercise to have three scenarios and three different places, three concepts. That's how it's organized.

**GA:** Describe the three parts in more detail?

**Portzamparc:** Functionally there are three bays, each of them contains part of the common spaces, restaurant, theater, materials workshops, and things like that. Then you have three spatial concepts. One is organized around central void, a square, and is built in stone, wood and concrete. It is an additional method of construction. Another is organized not on the outside void but as an object in a three-dimensional situation, with a sort of glass greenhouse. This is composed of steel boxes. The third is organized as intersecting voids and solids in molded concrete and glass. It's three experiments and three types of materials and I think it's interesting to go from one to another. It's not important that the library is not closed off. In fact, when they asked me why the library wasn't closed off, I said that it would be interesting to walk one-hundred meters while experiencing the quiet of the library. The library and

*Island 1 (left) & Island 2 (right)*

*View of entrance*

で，どこにもオープンスペースはありませんでしたが，この2つのヴォイドを導入することで，内部は明るくなり，さらに重要なことには，3つの建物を空間的にも形態的にも別のものとすることができたことです。これが，変化をつくるという，次のアイディアにつながって行ったのです。はじめに，学校をできるだけニュートラルなものにして欲しいと頼まれました。つまり，白か灰色ということです。しかし学校のように多くの人々を収容する建物には適切であるとはいえません。建物の重要性がその存在の様相を決定的なものにすると思いました。特にこれから建築を学び始めようとする学生たちにとって，個性的な空間がとても強い印象を残すものであることもよく知っていました。空間そのものが建築の分野への恰好の入門書のようなものです。形態や空間構成が人の知覚にどのように働きかけるかを感じとることもできるでしょう。それは学業の過程で，ゆっくりと試行してゆくべき何かではありますが，この潜在的可能性を心におきながら，一人の建築家のヴィジョンではたぶんあまりに権威的になってしまうだろうとも感じていました。今日，われわれのもとにはただ一つの建築，ただ一つの可能性，ただ一つのスタイルがあるのではなく，数多く存在するわけですから，それぞれのアイランドを別々の建築家に設計してもらおうかとも考えま

した。同僚2人に，2つのアイランドを頼みたいと思ったのですが，コンペに対応するには複雑にすぎ，経費や時間のことを解決するには時間がなく，結局自分でやることにしました。3つのシナリオ，3つの異なった敷地，3つのコンセプトを一人で担当するという練習問題みたいなものでした。と，こんなふうに組立てられていったわけです。

**GA：**その3つのアイランドはどんなものになるわけですか。

**ポルザンパルク：**機能的には3つのベイに分かれ，それぞれに，共有空間，レストラン，シア

ター，材料ワークショップなどが収容されています。次に3つの空間的なコンセプトがあります。一つは中央のヴォイド──広場を囲んで構成され，石と木とコンクリートの建物で，加算的な構法であるわけです。もう一つは外部空間であるヴォイドのうえに構成するのではなく，一種のガラスで包まれた温室のような，三次元のオブジェで，スティール・ボックスで構成されています。3つ目はヴォイドと面の交差として構成され，型枠コンクリートとガラスでできています。三種類の実験，三種類の材料があるわけで，一つの空間から次の空間に移っていく

the workshops on the top are devoted to research. In the other two, the levels can be mixed.

**GA:** The three, then, are totally separate structures?

**Portzamparc:** Yes, but they are connected by outside corridors.

**GA:** What about the in-between spaces?

**Portzamparc:** The pond and the cloister are interesting spaces because there are exhibition and assessment halls, and an amphitheater. It could welcome interaction

with the public outside. There is also a small building for competitions, and a place for sculpture in the courtyard. Nearby is a workshop for models and plastic arts.

The idea was that it would function in the end as a whole because of the clarity of the three islands. But each of them is a particular experience. Of course, some experience of the Cité de la Musique and the School of the Beaux-arts are in evidence here. The problem of having 1000 students

in the same place, and of introducing the experience of diverse places, was interesting. Meeting places are important also. Separate places don't create any functional problems. Instead of saying you have one place where everyone is gathered, as in Tschumi's proposal, my project proposes a network of places, leaving the possibility, not of one big gathering, but of smaller groups and families to coexist. I think this is more like how a school actually functions.

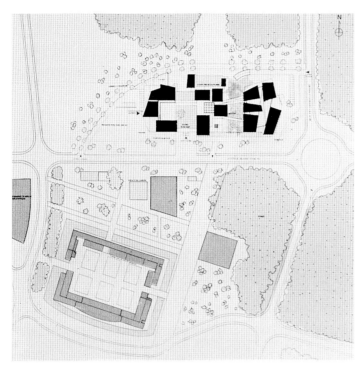

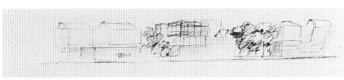

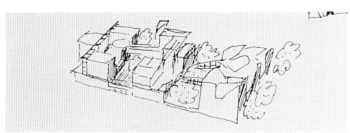

*Competition panels*

*Studies*

のは楽しいと思いますよ。図書館が閉鎖的でないのは重要なことではありません。事実、なぜ隔離されていないのか質問されましたが、私は反対に100mも図書館の静けさを味わいながら歩くのは楽しいのではないかと答えました。最上階の図書室とワークショップは研究者用です。他の2つでは、各階の用途はミックスしています。

**GA:** では、3つは完全に分離した建物であるわけですね。

**ポルザンパルク:** そうです。でも外側を廊下が繋いでいます。

**GA:** 各アイランドの間にある空間についてはいかがですか。

**ポルザンパルク:** 池と回廊がある空間は、展示ホールや審査用ホールがあり、アンフィシアターがあり、とても楽しいものです。外との交流の場としても利用できるし、コンペのときのための小さな建物もあり、中庭には彫刻を飾る場所もあります。すぐ近くには模型や造形芸術のためのワークショップがあります。

明快に3つのアイランドに分かれているために、最後には一つの統一体として機能するという考えです。しかしその一つ一つが特有の経験

なのです。もちろん、音楽都市やボザールでのいくつかの経験もここには含まれています。1000人もの生徒を一つの場所に収容し、多彩な場所の経験へ導くという課題は面白いものでした。人々が集える場所も大切です。3つに分かれているということ自体には何の問題もありません。チュミの計画案のように、誰もが集まれる一つの場所の代わりに、私の案は、大きな集団ではなく、いくつかの小さなグループや家族が共生できるような場のネットワークを提案しているのです。この方が実際の学校のありかたに適合していると思います。

# Extension of the Palais des Congrès
## ポルト・マイヨーの会議場増築

Supervisor: Chambre de Commerce et d'Industrie de Paris   Client: Société Immobilière du Palais des Congrès   Program: extension of the Palais des Congrès; new exhibition places, offices and a new 550-seat lecture hall   Design year: competition winning entry. 1994 (studies in progress)   Structural system: reinforced concrete   Area: 13,606 m² (re-arranged area), 46,915 m² (new area)   Engineer: Setec Travaux Publics et Industriels   Quantity surveyor: Atec

WITHDRAWN

Porte Maillot, Paris, France

*Elevation onto Porte Maillot*

*CG: perspectives showing different color schemes for illumination at night*

**GA:** Tell me what the basic goals for this project were.

**Portzamparc:** Port Maillot is a problem about a gateway to Paris. I am attempting to rejuvenate the presence of this large square.

**GA:** Is the project mostly about exterior rehabilitation?

**Portzamparc:** No, it's not just about the exterior. The problem comprises a series of new facilities. New exhibition spaces, more office space for administrative purposes, and a new congress hall for 600 people. I wanted the building to mark the entrance to Paris, even though it is to one side of grand processional axis. The gesture is a very simple one. I began with a large wall that cants forward, so as to leave more space in front. At first I wanted the space to be transparent but then I realized that there were to be exhibition halls right behind that precluded too much light. We were asked to add a congress hall. I decided right off that to place this in the center would create too formal and static a composition for the entry, so I placed it to the side and protruding a little from the facade. I chose a conical shape for this. But the problem of resolving this protrusion through the glass facade became very complicated. Then one night I decided to incline the whole in extension of the difficult shape of the congress hall, which made it possible to keep the conical presence. It has been turned and is no longer outside the building, but inside the building. The existing building had balconies on the facade of the lower block. I decided not to use balconies. I proposed a series of staircases stepping down from one big balcony. Instead of an entrance, we have stairs everywhere. With this combination I create a large parvis, the place in front, and generous surfaces. I was also careful not to break up any of the existing parts so as to respect the construction budget and schedule.

**GA:** This canted form is something you have used before, in your conservatory at La Villette for instance.

**Portzamparc:** Well here at Maillot, the role of the wall is not the same as at La Villette. The solution came from the site, by manipulation. But at one point I realized that there is a relationship between the cornice of the Paris Opera dance school and the big cornice or wall of the conservatory of the Cité de la Musique. Here, the idea of the wall became the whole building. Subconsciously, it may well follow my earlier designs. Maybe I already knew the effectiveness of reversal, and this is in my thinking about architecture.

**GA:** Now that we've discussed your formal

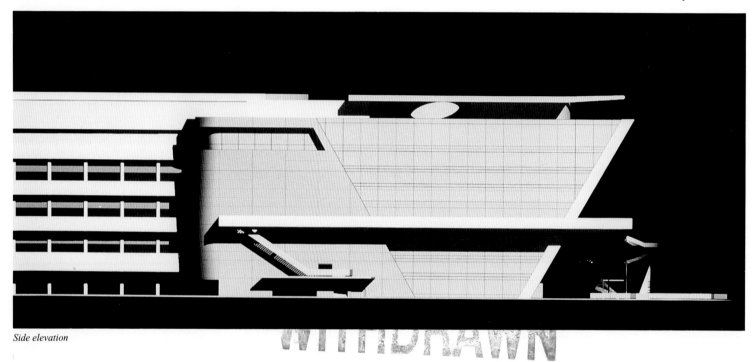

*Side elevation*

**GA：**このプロジェクトの基本的な目標はどのようなものですか。

**ポルザンパルク：**ポルト・マイヨーというのはパリに通じる門の一つです。この大きな広場の存在を活性化させようというものです。

**GA：**外部の改修を中心としたものですか。

**ポルザンパルク：**外部だけのものではありません。一連の新しい施設の問題もありました。新しい展示スペース，管理事務スペースの増築，600人収容できる会議ホールなどの建設も含まれています。パリへの基軸線の一方だけを構成するものではありますが，建物に門を思わせるような感じを付与したいのです。そのジェスチュアはとても単純なものです。前部になるべく大きな空きがとれるように，前方に傾斜する大きな壁から設計を始めました。最初は空間をできるだけ透明感のあるものにしたかったのですが，そのあとで，壁のすぐ背後に，あまり陽を浴びせてはいけない展示ホールがくることに気づきました。会議ホールを加えることも頼まれました。このホールを中央に配置すると，あまりにフォーマルで，入口部分が静的になってしまうので，少し端に寄せ，正面から少し突き出すことにしました。円錐形にしましたが，ガラス面からこの形を突出させることは非常に複雑なことになります。そしてある夜，すべての形を会議ホールの難しい形に合わせて傾斜させることに決めたので，デザインは簡素化され，円錐形を残すこともできました。それは向きを変えて，外側にではなく，建物の内側に位置することになりました。既存建物には，低い方のブロックの正面にバルコニーがついていましたが，今回は，バルコニーを全く使わないことに決め，代わりに一つの大きなバルコニーから降りてくる階段をつけることにしました。エントランスの代わりにあらゆるところに階段があるのです。この組合せによって，大きなパーヴィス――建物前の場所や広い面をつくることができました。また，工費と工期を守るためには重要でしたので，古い部分を壊さないように慎重に作業を進めました。

**GA：**この傾斜した形は以前にも使っていらっしゃいますね。たとえばラ・ヴィレットの音楽学校など。

**ポルザンパルク：**しかしこのマイヨーでの壁の傾斜の目的はラ・ヴィレットの場合とは違っています。ここでは敷地の，その巧妙な操作が目的です。しかしある点で，オペラ座舞踊学校のコーニスと，音楽都市の音楽学校の大きなコーニス，つまり2つの壁の間には関係があることに気づきました。ここでは，この壁のアイディアが建物全体になったのです。ですから，無意識のうちに以前のデザインに従っているのかもしれません。私は何かを逆転することの効果を既に知っていたのかもしれず，それが私の建築に対する考え方のなかにもあるのです。

**GA：**形態上の意図についてうかがったわけで

intentions; what about your attitude toward the street and the grand processional axis?

**Portzamparc:** Of course, all through the design, I was also thinking about what would happen outside, the perception of the gateway and this big square for cars, situated on the grand processional axis from the Louvre to La Défense. It was important for me to avoid a circular figure. The circle is not that important a factor. In fact, although you have this circle or star shape, the place is obviously a cross. It is not important to me to follow the circle that exists here with my own circle. The thing that matters is the speed of this great axis. I wanted to emphasize this speed and wanted the scale of the new building to create a scale for the void in front. The building as it stands is unsure of its dimensions; it is almost trying to be smaller. But I think this building needs a certain sureness of dimension and scale to respond to this huge space with cars flashing by.

**GA:** Why did you set the line straight instead of having a curve according to the present shape of the place?

**Portzamparc:** I don't think a curve has any topological raison d'être. None of the surrounding buildings follow this ellipse. In fact, sixty years ago there was no ellipse here at all, just a gateway to Paris. The curve was introduced to organize the space but I think it is rather weak. To me it is important, when designing something with a circle, to achieve something like an envelope. Here there is nothing to suggest this. I don't think it is in keeping with or adding to the dynamic of the space. You have the axis, you have the image, you have the space, the speed. It is important that the building keep these things together through its presence. The building creates a space that is very big. The space is not real, yet it exists by virtue of the building. Because the building is well positioned and has a strong presence you become conscious of that space in front of it and around it. You have a form which is the form of Paris—a small in miniature. That's why the building's going to be clearly visible from a fast car.

**GA:** Is this going to be illuminated like your Bandai project in Tokyo?

**Portzamparc:** Yes. It represents a continuation of my work with lighting in the concert hall of Cité de la Musique and my ideas for my project in Tokyo. The building is lit from below and will create changing colors for events or at night, which could be quite interesting. It is still in the project stage, and we are not sure when we can build, since there are problems with the building codes.

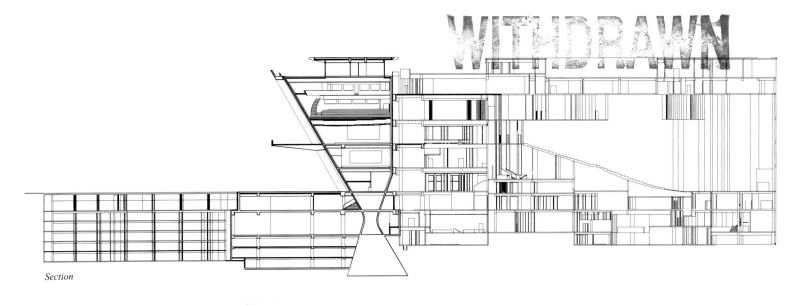

*Section*

すが，街路や軸線に対する態度についてはいかがですか。

**ポルザンパルク：**もちろん，デザインしている間ずっと，外部で何が発生するか，門としての知覚，ルーヴルとラ・デファンスを結ぶ大きな軸線上にある自動車交通のためのこの広い場所について考えてきました。私には円形を避けることが重要でした。円形は，構成要因とするだけの重要性を持っていません。ここには円や星形がありますが実際にはこの場所は十字形なのです。既存の円に，私が考えている円を合わせることはそれほど重要ではなかったのです。実際に問題なのは，この大きな軸線には速度があることです。この速度を強調することと，建物前のヴォイドに，あるスケールをつくりだすような大きさを与えたかったのです。今，そこに建っている建物の大きさではまだ不十分で，現実よりも小さく見えてしまう傾向があります。反対に，車がかなりの速度で通り過ぎるこの巨大な場所と均衡をとるには，建物には確かな大きさとディメンションが必要だと思うのです。

**GA：**現在の広場の形に従って曲線を使う代わりに，直線にしたことには何か理由があるのですか。

**ポルザンパルク：**広場の曲線はトポロジカルな根拠があって存在しているのではないと思うのです。この楕円に沿った形で建っている建物は一つもありません。事実，60年前にはここには楕円は存在せず，パリに通じる門が一つあっただけです。この曲線はこの場所を組立てるためにできたものですが，これは弱すぎると思います。円を使って何かをデザインするとき私が大切にしていることは，何かを包み込むようにすることです。ここにはそれが全く見あたりません。この空間のダイナミズムを維持するものも，添加するものもあるとは思えません。軸線があり，イメージがあり，空間があり，速度があります。建物はその存在を通して，これらの事を一緒に保持しつづけることが大切なのです。この建物はとても大きな空間をつくり上げます。その空間は現実のものではありませんが，建物のゆえに存在するのです。建物の巧みな位置そしてその壮大な存在感ゆえに，建物の前や周りに，そうした空間の存在を意識させられるのです。パリを型どったミニチュアの形があります。スピードを出している車から建物が知覚できるようにするためです。

**GA：**この建物もまた東京のバンダイみたいに照明されるのですか。

**ポルザンパルク：**ええ。このプロジェクトは音楽都市のコンサートホールや東京のプロジェクトで用いた照明のアイディアに続くものです。建物は下からライトアップされ，イヴェントの際や夜間には色彩が変化していきます。とても楽しいものになると思います。今はプロジェクトの段階で，建築基準法の問題があり，まだいつ着工できるかどうか確かではありません。

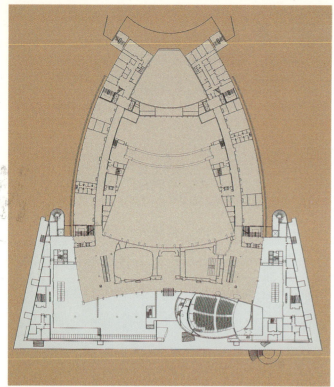

*Level 6.5 plan*

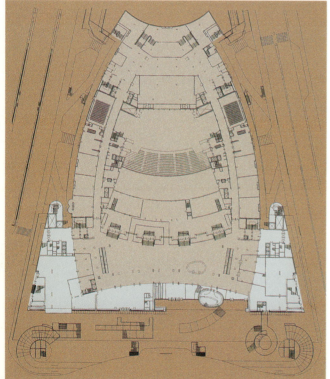

*Ground floor plan*

*CG*

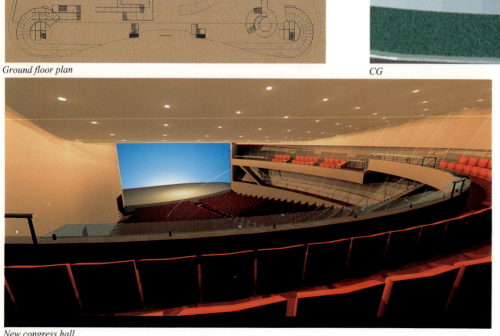

*New congress hall*

*New congress hall*

CHRISTIAN DE PORTZAMPARC
クリスチャン・ド・ポルザンパルク

| | |
|---|---|
| 1944 | Born in Casablanca, Morocco. French Nationality<br>モロッコのカサブランカに生まれる。フランス国籍 |
| 1969 | Diploma in Architecture at École Normale Supérieure des Beaux-Arts, Paris<br>エコール・デ・ボザール卒業 |
| 1975 | French New Architectural Program (PAN VII) awarded<br>by the French Ministry of Housing and Transport<br>フランス政府設備運輸省よりフランス新建築賞(PAN VII) |
| 1988 | "Équerre d'Argent" awarded by the Architectural Publishing Group<br>Le Moniteur, for the Dance School of the Paris' Opera<br>ル・モニトゥール建築出版グループより<br>パリ・オペラ座舞踊学校に対し銀の三角定規賞 |
| 1989 | Named "Commandeur de L'Ordre des Arts et des Lettres"<br>by the French Minister of Culture<br>フランス政府文化省より，芸術，文芸勲章コマンドゥール章 |
| 1990 | Grand Prix d'Architecture de la Ville de Paris<br>awarded by the Mayor of Paris<br>パリ市長よりパリ市建築大賞 |
| 1992 | Medal of the French Academy of Architecture<br>フランス建築アカデミーよりメダル受賞 |
| 1993 | Grand Prix Nationale de L'Architecture awarded<br>by the French Ministry of Housing and Transport<br>フランス政府設備運輸省より建築大賞 |
| 1994 | Pritzker Architectural Prize awarded by the Hyatt Foundation<br>ハイヤット財団よりプリツカー建築賞 |
| 1995 | "Équerre d'Argent" awarded by the Architectural Publishing Group<br>Le Moniteur, for the City of Music<br>音楽都市に対し銀の三角定規賞 |

Members of the Atelier Christian de Portzamparc

Christian de Poartzamparc, François Barberot, Bruno Barbot, Céline Barda, Bertrand Beau, Wilfrid Bellecour, Olivier Blaise, François Calliaud, Jean Charles Chaulet, François Chochon, Karol Claverie, Kaan Coskun, Bruno Durbeco, Paul Guilleminot, Julie Howard, Benoît Juret, Florent Leonhardt, Jean François Limet, Sam Mays, Marie Elisabeth Nicoleau, Etienne Pierres, Laurent Pierre, Etienne Pierres, Olivier Souquet, Johanna Wauquiez, Lea Xu

Artists: Christian Boltansky, Pierre Buraglio, Aurelie Nemours, Georges Noel, Yann de Portzamparc, Antonio Semerano (Cité de la Musique, West Part);
Louis Dandrel, Yann de Portzamparc (Cité de la Musique, East Part)
Interior designers: Franck Hammoutene, museum and museography; Elizabeth de Portzamparc, café de la musique; Véronique Branchut, RMN shop (Cité de la Musique, East Part)
Architect of the initial project: Rivet et Lassen (Rue Nationale, Rehabilitation Palulos, first and second phase, 1963 and 1964)

Photographic credits—Provided by Christian de Portzamparc (Nicolas Borel) : pp. 101, 103, 104, 105 below, 118–9, 122–3, 129, 131, 137, 142, 143, 147, 150, 151, 152

GAドキュメント・エクストラ 04 ＜クリスチャン・ド・ポルザンパルク＞
1995年11月27日発行／企画・編集・撮影：二川幸夫／インタヴュー：二川由夫／デザイン：細谷巖／発行者：二川幸夫
制作：ジーエー・デザインセンター／印刷・製本：大日本印刷株式会社／発行：エーディーエー・エディタ・トーキョー／東京都渋谷区千駄ヶ谷3-12-14
TEL：03-3403-1581／FAX：03-3497-0649／禁無断転載／ISBN4-87140-224-X C1352